From Revenue Sharing to Deficit Sharing

American Governance and Public Policy

A SERIES EDITED BY

Barry Rabe and John Tierney

This series examines a broad range of public policy issues and their relationship to all levels of government in the United States. The editors welcome serious scholarly studies and seek to publish books that appeal to both academic and professional audiences. The series showcases studies that illuminate the successes, as well as the problems, of policy formulation and implementation.

From Revenue Sharing to Deficit Sharing

General Revenue Sharing and Cities

Bruce A. Wallin

GEORGETOWN UNIVERSITY PRESS / WASHINGTON, D.C.

Georgetown University Press, Washington, D.C. 20007
© 1998 by Georgetown University Press. All rights reserved.

10 9 8 7 6 5 4 3 2 1   1998

THIS VOLUME IS PRINTED ON ACID-FREE ⊚ OFFSET BOOK PAPER

Library of Congress Cataloging-in-Publication Data

Wallin, Bruce.
   From revenue sharing to deficit sharing : general revenue sharing
and the cities / Bruce Wallin.
     p.   cm. — (American governance and public policy)
   Includes index.
   1. Revenue sharing—United States. 2. Intergovernment fiscal
relations—United States. 3. Federal-city relations—United States.
I. Title.   II. Series.
HJ275.W25   1998
336.73—dc21
ISBN 0-87840-698-0 cloth   98-5662
ISBN 0-87840-699-9 paper

For Francis P. (Chip) and
Freda A. Wallin

Contents

List of Tables

Preface

The enactment of General Revenue Sharing (GRS) in 1972 was widely heralded as a revolutionary change in U.S. federal aid policy. Many analyzed its passage and scores more studied its impact at the state and local level, making it for a period *the* most scrutinized federal policy.

Yet no one wrote at length of the politics of its demise, or the broader implications of its life and death. General Revenue Sharing is too important a part of the history of federalism and federal aid to leave its entire story untold. The goal of this book is to remedy that oversight, and in the process to examine its relevance to the U.S. intergovernmental aid environment as the turn of the century approaches.

I felt a certain obligation to do this. In 1971–1972 I was a special assistant to the mayor in Trenton, New Jersey, in charge of city–federal relations. In this capacity I became extremely involved in the lobbying efforts on behalf of revenue sharing. Arriving for graduate school at Berkeley in the Fall of 1972, I sought funding to record the impressions of local chief executives as to the then-anticipated impact of the program; my experience in Trenton had made me skeptical of the expectations which had been enunciated in Washington. I conducted a follow-up survey in 1974, and the data found its way into both my Master's and Ph.D theses.

In 1978, I went to Washington to work at the U.S. Advisory Commission on Intergovernmental Relations (ACIR), where one of my tasks was to examine the case for the renewal of General Revenue Sharing in 1980. After teaching at the University of Wisconsin, Madison, where I conducted another survey to gauge ongoing program impact, I returned to the ACIR in 1985–1986 and witnessed the demise of the program. Soon back in academia, I surveyed the same cities once more to determine final uses of the funds and the impact of, and response to, its termination.

Thus I kept as abreast of the revenue-sharing experience as perhaps anyone. The devolution movement of the 1990s and the twenty-fifth anniversary of General Revenue Sharing's passage prodded me to write this book.

It is intended for many audiences. For some, like my students who have asked where they can find a history of revenue sharing, the book seeks to explain its politics and policy at both the federal and municipal levels of government. For others who are interested in understanding how the devolution emphasis matured, it offers a description of the unique and ironic role of GRS in its development. And finally, for those like me who are interested in fairness and policy reform, it makes the case for reconsideration of a program of federal unrestricted aid.

There are many to thank. The late Arthur Holland, former Mayor of Trenton, gave me a position of responsibility unexpected by someone my age. He also taught me the importance of being intellectually honest in the development and implementation of public policy and convinced me of the ability of elected officials to do good for people, to make their lives better. The late Aaron Wildavsky, my academic mentor, made me rethink my analysis of revenue sharing at every stage. It often wasn't my analysis that he disagreed with, but its presentation. He taught me how to conduct and present academic research. These men, each in his own way, had a huge impact on me, both personally and professionally, and I will never forget them.

George Break, professor of economics at Berkeley, and John Shannon, my supervisor at the ACIR, also played very important roles in the development of this research.

Several organizations offered research support that was ultimately crucial to the book. The Institute for Governmental Studies at the University of California, Berkeley, offered the resources to fund the early portion of the study. The University of Wisconsin's Department of Political Science funded additional survey work, while Northeastern University's Research and Scholarship Development Fund, and a leave from the College of Arts and Sciences, allowed the book to actually be written.

I owe a debt of gratitude to the many student researchers who have worked on various aspects of the study. Carole Botticelli, Lisa Holmes, and Ivy Hanson deserve particular mention.

Finally, a very important word of thanks to my wife Vickie and my daughter Anne—Vickie for her proofreading, ideas, and encouragement, and Anne for the inspiration one gets from the smile of an infant daughter.

The book is dedicated to my late parents, who more than anyone helped put me in the position to write this book, and who always encouraged independent thought.

1

Theories, Politics, and Policy

It could be said that it was the best of programs, and the worst of programs. The most popular federal aid program ever from the point of view of state and local officials, General Revenue Sharing was characterized as "a snake in the grass" by one member of Congress. Passage of the program of unrestricted aid was an anomaly, a break from the predominant categorical grant form, and its termination an aberration in that it is difficult to kill a federal program once it is enacted.

General Revenue Sharing produced strange alliances. It was championed by Republican President Richard Nixon from conservative Orange County, California, and fought for by African-American Congressman John Conyers, a Democrat who represented urban Michigan. Republican President Ronald Reagan, a former governor and self-proclaimed pro-state president, issued its death warrant, with assistance from Democratic Speaker of the House Tip O'Neill, who, perhaps forgetting his own observation that "all politics is local," called the program "silliness."

It was a unique program in that there remain disagreements over whether it was more surprising that the program was passed or that it was terminated; for most programs, either one or the other is clearly true. It was once deemed sound enough policy to justify at its inception the largest domestic federal aid program in history, later not sound enough to warrant even a scaled-back program. Reigning intellectual rationales of the late 1960s and early 1970s supported its passage, while the predominant paradigms of the 1980s justified its demise. It made sense politically in 1972, but not by the mid-1980s. It was a program that did not live up to the grand expectations of the donors, but met the more modest and realistic goals of the recipients. Once the subject of sixty-seven bills in one session of the senate alone, it died with barely a whimper.

The federal General Revenue Sharing program was as controversial as it is important to the history of both federalism and intergovernmental relations in the United States. Indeed, perhaps the only thing scholars agree on is that passage of the program of unrestricted federal aid to state and local governments was very significant, ranked as the second most important intergovernmental event of 1960–1980.[1]

Its history reveals much about changes in federal politics and policy over the past twenty years or so, including the increased importance of federal deficit reduction and the related but not totally resultant decline in the power of the intergovernmental lobby. Its passage in 1972 and termination in 1986 rather eerily bookend the peak year of federal aid to state and local governments for governmental purposes, 1978. Its ending ironically coincides with the shift from a majority of federal grant dollars going to governments to a majority going to individuals, for programs like Medicaid and Aid to Families With Dependent Children.[2]

This book is about the General Revenue Sharing program—why it passed, why cities used it the way they did, and why it died. But its story offers much more, including most importantly insight into federalism and intergovernmental politics, and the difficulty of enacting sound intergovernmental aid policy in a federal system, lessons relevant to the current emphasis on devolution. Revenue sharing's enactment and termination also parallel to a great extent the rise and fall of the state and local intergovernmental lobby in Washington. A closer look at its impact informs grant theory while reconfirming much of what has been known about municipal budgeting for some time. And while the program was ended, the rationale which underpinned it lingers, evidenced at the state level, in other nations, and even in thin disguise in newer national programs, both proposed and enacted.

GENERAL REVENUE SHARING IN CONTEXT

The fiscal stature of local governments in the American federal system underwent a rather remarkable transformation in the twentieth century. From the country's founding through the first World War, local governments financed and produced the bulk of the services demanded by a rapidly growing nation. Yet by the 1970s some commentators characterized large cities in particular as little more than fiscal wards of the federal government.

As late as 1932, local government expenditures accounted for 47.3 percent all U.S. public outlays, compared to 31.6 percent and 21.1 percent for the federal and state sectors, respectively (Table 1-1). Furthermore, local governments raised 52.3 percent of all public revenues that year, in contrast to federal collections of 25.6 percent and a state share of 22.1 percent (Table 1-2).

A look at the federal fiscal landscape only thirty-eight years later revealed great changes. Local government expenditures in 1970 had

TABLE 1-1
Government General Expenditures (in millions)

	1932			1970	
Federal	$4,261	31.6%	Federal	$208,190	54%
State	$2,829	21.1%	State	$85,055	22%
Local	$6,375	47.3%	Local	$92,522	24%

Source: U.S. Department of Commerce, Bureau of the Census, *Historical Statistics of the United States: Colonial Times to 1970* (Washington, DC: U.S. Government Printing Office, 1975): pp. 1123, 1130, 1134.

dropped to 17.8 percent of all governmental outlays in the United States. Between 1932 and 1970, the local percentage of all own source revenues in the federal system fell from the 52.3 percent in 1932, to 17.8 percent. Local government tax collections, which had provided nearly 70 percent of their total revenue in 1932 fell to 44 percent by 1970. Local revenue raising, and hence autonomy, had been seriously undermined.

There were many reasons for the dramatic turnaround. Local government's access to tax sources was (and is) in most cases limited by state law. As a result, local officials historically have had to rely on the ever-unpopular property tax. Citizen opposition to property tax hikes heightens elected officials' fears of tax competition, the threat that an increase in local taxes will drive those homeowners, landlords, and businesses at the margin into neighboring lower-tax jurisdictions. This has been especially true for older central cities. While studies of the actual effect of property tax burden on intercity moves have been inconclusive, elected officials nonetheless came to view the property tax rate as a barometer of the economic health of their city, and one

TABLE 1-2
Revenues from Own Sources (in millions)

	1932			1970	
Federal	$2,234	25.6%	Federal	$205,562	61.6%
State	$2,274	22.1%	State	$68,691	20.6%
Local	$5,381	52.3%	Local	$59,557	17.8%

Source: U.S. Department of Commerce, Bureau of the Census, *Historical Statistics of the United States: Colonial Times to 1970* (Washington, DC: U.S. Government Printing Office, 1975): pp. 1121, 1122, 1129, 1130.

of the factors relating to locational choice which they could control. Meanwhile, suburbanization and subsequent incorporation of land areas surrounding cities took away geographic expansion as a source of new property tax revenue for many jurisdictions. These property tax-related considerations—both political and geographic—seriously impaired the ability of many cities to raise the revenue adequate to their task. At the same time, cities came to be increasingly inhabited by lower income residents, especially in central cities, a population which places extra demands on public services.

It was under these circumstances that local governments, and cities in particular, embraced increased financial assistance from their state governments and from Washington, even with the resultant loss in local control. In 1932, municipal governments relied on federal and state aid for 9.2 percent of their revenues; by 1971–1972, 33 percent of all city revenues came from these other levels of government (Table 1-3). By 1976–1977, city government reliance on intergovernmental aid grew to 39.6 percent of their revenue.[3] Clearly, then, local officials had moved from a position of financial independence to one of extreme dependence on aid from other levels of government.

Financial planning is difficult when such a large amount of city revenue is to be determined in a different political arena. City governments adapted as best they could. While not a perfect response, the need for effective intergovernmental lobbying led to an explosion of new positions ("office of grants coordinator," etc.) in city halls across America.[4] The importance of stable intergovernmental relations became paramount.

Most federal grants intended for local governments were at one time channeled through the states for an ultimately local impact. During the post-World War II period an important change occurred: the federal government increasingly bypassed the states to give grants directly to local governments. While most of the intergovernmental aid going to local governments has always come from their state governments,

---

TABLE 1-3
City Government Revenue (in millions)

1932		1971–72	
General Revenue	$2,677	General Revenue	$34,998
Intergovt. Revenue	$245	Intergovt. Revenue	$11,528
as percentage	9.2%	as percentage	32.9%

Source: U.S. Department of Commerce, Bureau of the Census, *1982 Census of Governments* vol. 6, no. 4 (Washington, DC: U.S. Government Printing Office, 1985): p. 38.

federal grants-in-aid were the fastest growing revenue source in the 1970s. Federal aid to cities grew from providing 7.5 percent of all city revenue in 1972 to 13.8 percent in 1977.

Why the new connection? One of the explanations for what came to be known as city "end runs" around state governments to seek financial support from Washington was what city executives perceived as a decreasing responsiveness of state legislatures to big-city needs. Suburbanization combined with reapportionment meant increased Republicanism in many state legislatures. This changing composition of state representation weakened the political position of Democrat-ruled urban areas, diluting the urban impact of federal aid passed through states. The new federal aid approach eventually came to be known as "Creative Federalism" and was also politically rational from the point of view of federal elected officials, especially Democrats. Aid to the cities rekindled loyalties and produced political debts which could be called due on election day. The electoral strength of cities was viewed as important to Congressional candidates and presidential aspirants.[5]

What allowed the federal government such largesse? Clearly there were some responsibilities that it was forced to accept during the Great Depression. But many observers of the changing intergovernmental scene argue that the expansion was most broadly made possible by the strength of the federal income tax. The U.S. Advisory Commission on Intergovernmental Relations (ACIR) reported in 1970:

> An increasingly interdependent economy, a vastly superior jurisdictional reach and a near monopoly of the income tax enable the Congress to raise far more revenue at far less political risk than can all of the State and local officials combined. While the careers of many State and local officials have been wrecked by courageous decisions to increase taxes, similar action at the Federal level is seldom necessary and rarely if ever fatal to a political career.[6]

The superior revenue-raising ability of a federal income tax, with a broader reach, provisions for withholding, a progressive rate structure fueled by inflation, and unfettered by tax competition concerns, produced the "dividend" to share with state and local governments. Increasingly aware of this revenue superiority, interest groups representing cities increasingly turned their lobbying attention to Washington, where they also learned that fighting one battle was more efficient than fighting fifty.[7]

The great majority of these federal grants-in-aid were of a categorical nature, grants which have very specific programmatic restrictions on the use of the funds. In fiscal year 1970, for example, 95 percent of all federal grant money had specific programmatic aims.[8] Thus while on the one hand it would appear to be a politician's dream to be able to spend money raised by another level of government, these grants individually and collectively resulted in a loss of autonomy for city officials and often influenced (some would say distorted) their priorities. Further, most of these categorical grant programs required application and reporting, raising administrative costs and ultimately producing lobbying activity aimed at successful review—a situation negatively characterized as state and local tax dollars chasing federal tax dollars.

It was a reaction to exactly this trend toward imposition of federal program priorities on state and local governments at a high administrative cost that led President Nixon to propose a New Federalism. In his 1971 State of the Union Message, Nixon announced the philosophy behind a new approach to grants-in-aid:

> If we put more power in more places, we can make the government more creative in more places. . . . The further government is from the people, the stronger government becomes and the weaker people become. And a nation with a strong government and a weak people is an empty shell. . . . Local government is the government closest to the *people*, it is most responsive to the individual *person*. . . . (emphasis in original)[9]

The Administration's "new American revolution" in fiscal federalism got underway with the passage and implementation of the "State and Local Fiscal Assistance Act of 1972"—most widely known as the General Revenue Sharing program. Enacted in October 1972, the plan earmarked nearly seven billion dollars of federal income for annual distribution to state and local governments. Recipient governments were basically free to spend the revenue as they wished. In another important break with tradition, the funds were transferred automatically, by formula, without annual appropriation by Congress. Initially authorized for a five-year period, the program was extended in 1976 through 1980 and was reauthorized in December 1980 for local governments, while the state governments' share was essentially eliminated.[10] Reauthorized for local governments again in 1983, the program was ended in 1986.

The concept of a new American revolution referred chiefly to the intended shift in decision-making power from the federal government to the state and local level that would accompany the revenue shift—from Washington back to "the people." It was anticipated that local decision making in particular would be rejuvenated by receipt of revenue sharing funds, and that local officials would at last be able to react more readily and appropriately to the particular problems facing their jurisdictions, free from the types of restrictions surrounding most existing categorical grant programs. Other goals of the program included the ambitious economic objectives of general fiscal relief and a redistribution of resources. Some hoped that such local governmental fiscal relief would be transformed into local property tax relief, while others anticipated a stimulation of local initiatives in various program areas.

ORIGINS OF THIS STUDY

Given the tremendous importance of intergovernmental aid to cities at the time, this study began as an evaluation of the impact of General Revenue Sharing on large cities, using surveys of city chief executives in two states, California and New Jersey. There were two strong reasons for focusing on the program's impact on urban areas. First, the plight of hard-pressed local governments had been the most often-used and most convincing rationale for the program's initial passage, and concerns over local fiscal conditions were essential to the renewal debates. The state share of General Revenue Sharing had become endangered long before the local share was in jeopardy. Second, proposed cutbacks in Great Society programs in Nixon's fiscal year 1974 budget added a new dimension—uncertainty—to decisions made on the local use of General Revenue Sharing funds, forcing officials in some instances to consider choosing between continuation of these programs using revenue sharing funds and termination. Thus it became important not only to analyze the impact of revenue sharing, but to compare its local uses with the kinds of priorities found in the federal domestic programs of the 1960s. Later surveys sought to record chief executives' impressions of the continuing impact of the program and the effect of its termination.

Thus the study began most broadly as an analysis of the impact of General Revenue Sharing on cities, as perceived by local chief executives. The word "analysis" is used rather than "evaluation" for good reason: to evaluate a program one must have a clear indication of that program's goal(s) or objective(s).[11] Revenue sharing had many. Patrick Larkey compiled what he termed a simple list of stated objectives for General Revenue Sharing:

Stated Objectives for General Revenue Sharing

1. To reduce the direct involvement of the federal government in domestic problems.

2. To reduce the amount of "red tape" associated with federal domestic programs.
3. To stimulate the creation and expansion of innovative local programs.
4. To increase the influence of each citizen as to how the money is used, make government more responsive to taxpayer pressures, and enhance accountability.
5. To increase the involvement of local citizens in governmental decision-making processes.
6. To stimulate the development of effective and responsive planning and priority-setting mechanisms at the local level.
7. To help improve the management and administration of state and local governments, including the consolidation of units.
8. To allocate to the states and local governments on a permanent basis a portion of the very productive and highly "growth-elastic" receipts of the federal government.
9. To compensate for the federal government's use of the best tax sources.
10. To use more equitable tax systems by substituting federal for state and local taxes as a way of financing state and local services.
11. To provide relief to state and local taxpayers.
12. To stabilize spiraling local tax rates.
13. To moderate the variation that now exists in state and local tax rates and public service levels.
14. To improve the quality and quantity of services offered at the local level and to equalize their distribution.
15. To redistribute resources among states and localities so as to enable the poorer ones to raise the level of public services they provide.
16. To alleviate some of the intense fiscal pressures on local, and particularly urban, governments.[12]

Never has one program provided such a clear example of policy goals that are multiple, vague, and conflicting. How a program could "increase the influence of each citizen" is not at all clear, while the "creation and expansion of innovative local programs" would seem to weaken its use for substantial "relief to state and local taxpayers."

Given the lack of a clear goal, the study began with a focus on the question of whether or not the local impact of the program approached the broadest goals implied by President Nixon's pronouncements; that is, given the decentralization of resources and power, and the publicity attendant to a major new federal program,

- was there a "burst of creative energy" at the local level?
- was decision making rejuvenated by an upsurge in citizen participation?
- did revenue sharing funds enable local officials to better and more creatively respond to the particular needs of their cities?

These issues fit into one all-encompassing question: what difference did the General Revenue Sharing program make to cities? That is, other than the obvious fiscal effect (more money), were budgeting processes and/or outcomes involving revenue-sharing funds any different than budgeting decisions involving locally raised revenue? And why were decisions made as they were?

At its inception the leading hypothesis of the research was that neither the process of determining the use of these funds, including the influences of its various participants, nor the resultant outcomes would vary considerably from the operation and results of traditional municipal budgeting. The chief theoretical basis for this hypothesis was the positive theory of municipal resource-allocation processes, as described by Crecine, among others.[13] Two other bodies of literature offered additional support to the particular contention that expenditures of revenue-sharing funds would to a great extent resemble the expenditure patterns which result from customary budgetary politics: the economic theory of grants-in-aid and the then-growing body of literature on the politics of intergovernmental aid.[14]

RELEVANT THEORIES

The Positive Theory of Municipal Budgeting

The hypothesis of unspectacular impact was, as noted, most directly a product of application of the positive theory of municipal budgeting. Simply stated, the theory suggests that due to the balanced-budget constraint and limited revenue-raising ability, the local budgeting process is highly structured and routinized, dominated by the chief executive, and relatively insulated from the environment. The theory further suggests that the resulting budgetary outcomes tend to vary incrementally from the previous year's budget.

Aaron Wildavsky's study of budgeting at the federal level found that process well-structured, with the roles of participants clearly understood.[15] The fact that municipal governments must adopt budgets which at least approximately balance revenues and expenditures dictates an even more defined approach than one in which such an equation is desired but not required.

The municipal budget process begins with a determination by the chief executive of what a realistic revenue increase for the city might be. He or she must consider increases or decreases in federal and state aid; projected growth in property and other tax bases; and finally, what increase in the property tax rate, if any, would be politically acceptable. A letter from the chief executive is then usually sent to the agency or department heads setting a "target increase figure"—it asks, for example, that budget requests not exceed a 5 percent increase over the previous year's allocation. While the letter sets a tone for the year's budgeting, agency heads at the municipal level, like their counterparts in Washington, consider their role to be that of advocate for increased expenditures in their program area.[16] They therefore often play budget games, such as requesting more than they actually need or expect, hoping that the inflated figure will provide a cushion against expected chief executive cuts. Should the requested figure actually survive, it is the rare agency head who could not find some use for the "bonus."

It is the chief executive's task to reconcile the agency demands with projected revenue, usually acting as budget cutter in a micro sense while led by the macro role of budget balancer. The chief executive subsequently sends the budget to the city council, over whom he or she enjoys a distinct resource advantage. Chief executives customarily have a much larger staff at their disposal than do members of the council, who also are often part-time. It is, however, the fact that the budget presented is in balance that most results in executive dominance of the process.

City council members, much like members of Congress, realize that deriving benefits for their constituents in the budget can aid their chances of reelection, and therefore they often seek to add expenditure items or at least to avoid cuts. But unlike their counterparts at the federal level, should members of the council wish to make changes in the budget, they must adjust both expenditures and revenue. Should they wish a net addition to the proposed budget, they would have to face the political hurdle of increasing taxes or cutting funds from some other expenditure area, a responsibility they would rather leave in the office of the mayor or city manager. The role of the city council in budgeting has thus not surprisingly come to be characterized as that of a rubber stamp. The importance (power) of executive preparation of the budget has also been documented at the similarly balanced-budget restrained state government level.[17] But local chief executives have the most power. And all other things being equal, the fewer the resources, the fewer the alternatives, the greater this power is.

Arnold Meltsner's path-breaking study of municipal budgeting in Oakland found that city managers in particular view their role as that of professional bureaucrat rather than politician, and so attempt to keep the budget process hidden from the potential unsettling effects of public intervention.[18] Citizen pressure is viewed as mostly affecting budget decisions through the revenue constraint; that is, the willingness of citizens to tolerate an increase in their tax burden will affect the overall level of resources available to the city. This factor is taken into account by the chief executive when he or she drafts the budget letter, but citizen pressure rarely exerts itself during the ensuing budget process and therefore does not often affect allocations among agency accounts.

How, then, are specific citizen demands met? Patrick Larkey explains:

> A great deal of the "pressure/accommodation behavior" (i.e., the organization's negotiations and adaption to its external environment) takes place through alterations in programmatic content (e.g., which roads get fixed and how they are fixed or where the tennis courts are built) without affecting allocation levels (i.e., account category–functional–proportions).[19]

Meltsner and Wildavsky similarly concluded about city budgeting:

> The *operating* budget is insulated from the environment. . . . If social scientists want to ascertain how, if at all, environmental demands are met, they will have to examine detailed allocations within city departments; whose street is repaired and what neighborhood gets the traffic signal are appropriate questions.[20]

The municipal budget process is for the most part an insider's game.

The decision rules used by the participants in the municipal budgetary process are similar to those Wildavsky described at the federal level.[21] Officials face extremely complex decisions; given the nature of most governmental services, it is very difficult to effectively measure outputs and nearly impossible to determine outcomes—the effect of city outputs on targeted situations. Participants not only lack information on the effectiveness of programs, but they also get less-than-clear signals from city residents on the demand for and satisfaction with various services. Yet decisions have to be made, and within a designated time frame. Rather than attempting to arrive at optimal decisions, these pressures result in "satisficing" behavior; determinations are satisfactory, they suffice, but are not ideal.[22] This situation results in the emergence of shared rules of thumb, the use of precedent (Wildavsky's "base"), and relatively even across-the-board increases or decreases (Wildavsky's "fair share").

While a pragmatic response to a problematic situation, incremental-ism in budgeting at all levels is also valued for its stabilizing effect, making it easier to compromise. Last year's appropriation is treated as a given and attention is focused on proposed changes. This not only simplifies decision making, but it also reduces uncertainty for all involved. Valued by many for these normative considerations, this incremental decision-making process most often produces incremental changes in budgetary allocations. It therefore obviously favors estab-lished agencies and programs over newcomers, and the most recent expenditure mix over any alternatives. Continued funding for old pro-grams will usually not cause internal or external discord. As Crecine notes, "Stability guarantees the ability to reach a decision—to come up with a balanced budget, while upsetting a minimal number of people and programs."[23] The predictive ability of last year's allocation in program areas has been well-documented.[24]

The balanced-budget requirement at the local level only accentuates this incremental nature of most budgeting. On the expenditure side, Meltsner and Wildavsky have noted that inflation leaves little budget-ary discretion for the chief executive:

> . . . it is easy to see that with the possibility of a two to three percent price increase for non-personnel costs, with standard salary increases of four to five percent, with slight increases in number of personnel, and with no increase in productivity, Oakland could have an eight percent growth rate in city expenditures each year without a marked increase in the level of service.[25]

A difficult process in stable economic times, city budgeting is even more challenging when inflation is high.

The other side of the budget equation, revenue raising, generally presents an even gloomier picture for city officials. The property tax, the predominant independent source of revenue for cities, is not the citizens' favorite.[26] The tax is the most visible and perhaps the most painful of all taxes, often requiring one or two lump-sum payments to local jurisdictions; the withholding aspect of the income tax and the diffuse nature of the sales tax reduce their perceived impact. While property tax rate increases are most objectionable to taxpayers, even greater tax liability due to an increase in property value and hence assessment, although producing a capital gain for the owner, also presents problems in that the asset is not a particularly liquid one—that is, it is not easily transferred into cash to pay a property tax bill. It is also a tax not necessarily related to income; in the extreme case, the property tax bill is due even if you're out of work. Meltsner and

Wildavsky observed that in 1969 Oakland, "City officials believe that raising the property tax would be an act of political suicide."[27] The rhetoric of almost all big-city mayors since then has consistently borne out this perception. And their concern has proved to be well-founded. It was, after all, property tax pressure which led to Proposition 13 and the so-called "Tax Revolt."[28]

To summarize, the municipal budgetary process has been found to be highly routinized, executive-dominated, and insulated from the environment. It involves an incremental process, producing incremental changes in budget allocations. It is this understanding of city budgeting which most strongly suggested that, despite expectations in Washington, the influx of General Revenue Sharing funds would not have much of an impact on either the allocation process or the budgetary outcomes customarily observed. This outcome was made even more likely by the fact that the funds to be received under the program could be spent on almost any activity, and that in effect they comprised only about 5–7 percent of general city revenue when the program started. In the fiscal year preceding arrival of revenue sharing funds, fy1972, municipal government revenue increases in the two states in the study, California and New Jersey, averaged 11 and 17 percent, respectively. Municipal budgeting is not likely to be dramatically altered by an influx of funds smaller than last year's increment.

Economic Theory

In speculating upon the response of local governments to various types of grants, economists use a model which uses price theory and treats cities as rational consumers.[29] In this view, resource allocation is "an 'optimizing process' in which a 'community welfare function' is posited and the 'governing body' attempts to maximize 'community welfare' for reasons of altruism, efficiency, or re-election."[30] While involving some rather strong assumptions and saying little about the process involved, the theory has had substantial policy impact, primarily through contrasting recipient response to matching categorical grants, to use of lump-sum, revenue sharing grants.[31] Ray Whitman and Robert Cline of the Urban Institute explain:

> Unconditional lump-sum grants can be viewed as a supplement to the resources available to the community. In terms of the budget constraint, a lump-sum grant shifts the constraint outward presenting budget officials with an increased set of opportunities to consume both public and private goods. A lump-sum grant would not affect the relative price of public versus private goods or the relative prices of outputs within the government budget.[32]

Lump-sum grants, then, have what is called an income effect; simply stated, they do not change the price of any particular good and therefore should not alter the attractiveness of providing any one program or service versus another. Categorical grants, on the other hand, in effect lower the price of a good (say, housing) for a local government, usually changing (increasing) local preference for that good.[33]

Given a normal community welfare function, then, a lump-sum grant like revenue sharing should not significantly alter the composition of the local budget, since the grant itself offers no economic incentive to produce (consume) any one type of good or service over another. While, again, the basic theory is lacking content relating to local decision-making processes and the broader range of incentives operative therein, the predicted result in terms of outcomes is not unlike that to be derived from application of the incremental view implied in the theory of municipal budgeting already discussed.

Economists have confronted some of the potential effects of internal incentives on municipal budgeting. Bureaucratic models of the impact of intergovernmental aid recognize "flypaper effects"—the tendency of grant money to "stick" in the public sector; that is, to be spent on government programs rather than be turned over to the local taxpayer through tax cuts. This approach stresses "government officials' and workers' pursuit of their own utility goals, rather than those of taxpayer–voters in the choice and operation of government programs."[34] These models nicely parallel the insulated nature of the positive theory of municipal budgeting as described by Crecine.

Intergovernmental Aid Theory

A third body of literature offered insight into expected city uses of revenue sharing funds and the specific question of whether General Revenue Sharing funds would likely be used to substitute for federal funds cut back in other grant-in-aid areas. This latter use would obviously result in different preferences than those customarily expressed through the local budgeting process; one of the leading reasons for many federal grants was the fact that local governments had failed to adequately fund program areas deemed to be in the national interest.[35] While not derived from as strong a theoretical and empirical foundation as the other two theories, principles from the literature on the politics of intergovernmental aid were relevant.

Ever since the wide dissemination of Robert Dahl's study of Mayor Lee and New Haven, mayors and city managers have courted federal aid as a potential resource.[36] The first of Deil Wright's "Pervasive IGR Rules for Local Officials" offers some simple advice: "Maximize federal and state dollar revenues and minimize local taxes."[37] Jeff Pressman, in his study of *Federal Programs and City Politics*, outlined the goals of grant recipients: "(1) attracting money; (2) achieving a steady flow of money; (3) autonomy; and (4) donor stability and support."[38]

Pressman's goals all suggest that it would not be in the best interests of city officials to use discretionary funds to replace any federal funds lost in Nixon's proposed fy1974 cutbacks in Great Society programs. In an unsteady, changing environment, local officials are not likely to want to give the federal government signals that they are willing to take over previously federally funded responsibilities. What could occur then is an interesting example of Pressman's "lack of a bargaining space" for federal and local officials, and a need to communicate in another fashion.[39] Local allocations of revenue sharing funds away from federal priority areas would be "sending a message to Washington."

This calculus is most directly a result of application of administrative theory; J.D. Thompson has noted the tendency of the rational organization to attempt to "buffer environmental influences," and in particular to "smooth out input" transactions. Organizations seek to reduce uncertainty, and the "bargaining through budgeting" suggested here is an attempt at what Thompson refers to as "the negotiation of an agreement for the exchange of performances in the future."[40]

In addition, Pressman notes an even more direct political rationale involved. Categorical grants involve guidelines which "provide an excellent scapegoat for local leaders who wish to avoid being held responsible for what may be an unpopular act. Even aggressive mayors benefit from the opportunity to say that 'the feds are making me do it' in backing a controversial cause."[41] It is difficult to justify spending local tax dollars in program areas which aid only a small segment of the population. For this reason of local politics, too, city chief executives might resist picking up any scaled-back responsibilities.

The desire to reduce uncertainty would also be directly relevant to the general allocation of revenue sharing funds. Local budget decisions in general were likely to be made with a wary eye toward the likelihood of a continuance of revenue sharing, a new form of aid without an established constituency either in Washington or locally. City officials thus would seek to avoid making any commitments which they later might find difficult to keep.

What happens when a highly hyped program meets an extremely routinized and stable budget process? Absent other incentives, the positive theory of municipal budgeting, supported by the economics and political science literature concerning intergovernmental grants, suggested that the existing process would dominate the new program, that program spending would vary only incrementally from that of the previous budget, and that substantial new spending would not likely appear in program areas traditionally funded by the federal government.

SURVEY DATA

The analysis of local dynamics and decisions relating to the impact of General Revenue Sharing on cities to be presented here relies in great part on survey work conducted in two states, supported by other studies. In October 1972, a questionnaire was sent out to city managers and mayors in sixty-seven California and thirty-three New Jersey cities (all with populations over 50,000, others Standard Metropolitan Statistical Area (SMSA) "central cities"—Appendix A). It sought to record the impressions of the city chief executives as to the anticipated impact of revenue sharing before arrival of the funds and, as it turned out, before the unveiling of President Nixon's fiscal year 1974 budget with its proposed cuts in categorical aid. A follow-up survey was conducted eighteen months later, asking chief executives to record their impressions of the program's actual impact. This time series perspective allows a critical examination of the effect of local variables on allocation decisions, as perceived by city chief executives. It appears that no other study of the impact of revenue sharing had this before–after perspective, and thus none can allow for a similar analysis. Interviews were also conducted with various participants in the local budget process in the two states to support the survey results.[42] Surveys were conducted again in 1984 to determine the continuing impact of the program, and in 1988 to gauge the effect of its termination.

There were basically four methodologies available to those interested in analyzing the impact of revenue sharing on cities. The first, statistical modeling, involves the use of fiscal, economic, and demographic data to attempt to determine what city expenditures would have been without the new funds and to compare them to actual expenditures, isolating the assumed effect of the federal dollars. This approach was weakened by the fact that there were no "control" cities, that is, cities which did not receive funds. An early analyst of revenue sharing's impact concluded that ". . . any analysis or interpretations about GRS that depend on fiscal effects analysis should be regarded as questionable."[43] Second, use-report data collected by the Department of Treasury were available, although the validity of these reports was highly suspect due to the incentive on the part of local officials to please federal officials and to prove that requirements were met. Third, the participant observer or "direct observation and analysis approach" relies on the presence of a researcher during the course of the activity under study. Finally, a study could rely on survey instruments and/ or interviews to record the impressions of the government officials involved in the decision-making process.[44]

The survey approach was chosen here for several reasons. The cost was lower, and the survey approach could produce more cases than the participant observer approach. Contrasted to statistical modeling, the survey and interview method is a better way to research the kinds of questions raised here, questions relating to how and why revenue-sharing expenditures were made as they were.

The methodology issue hinges on what the researcher is trying to accomplish. If the goal were to try to exactly account for revenue-sharing allocations by functional account, a study would not want to rely solely on the survey approach. Statistical modeling and analysis of budget trends, similar to those done by Larkey, would be more appropriate to that task. But the researcher is then left, as Larkey is, to wonder why outcomes were as they were.[45]

The study reported here relied on a survey of city chief executives since it has been so well-documented that they play the most important role in the budgeting process, and the impact of revenue sharing funds is basically a budgeting question. The chief executive is in the best position to view the overall process and gauge department, council, and citizen input. Further, it is the responsibility of the chief executive more than any other actor to keep abreast of the intergovernmental environment.

There were also particular strengths of the survey instruments used in this study, compared to others. First, the fact that the initial survey was conducted before the receipt of General Revenue Sharing funds allowed the establishment of a set of expectations on program impact. Comparing this data to that of the follow-up would test the executive-dominant model of municipal budgeting, while allowing for identification of actual community influence. This data could also be used to determine if communication between national and local officials regarding the expected impact of the program had been successful. Second, the surveys used here have an important conceptual strength over some of the other survey instruments used to study revenue sharing. Questions on broad uses of funds (e.g., expand services, capital expenditures, etc.) were kept separate from the issue of expenditures in specific functional areas (public safety, public works) to avoid problems of double-reporting (e.g., a new police car falls in both capital improvement and public safety categories in some studies, with no opportunity for the respondent to so designate). As Whitman and Cline have suggested, with respect to the use of surveys, "A well designed structure ... will yield results which, though subjective, are meaningful."[46]

Again, the most important point in defense of the survey approach used here is that it captured the attitudes, opinions, and beliefs of the most important actors in the municipal budgeting process, the chief executives, on the impact of revenue sharing in their cities. The study was not trying to measure the exact use of funds, but sought to analyze the process, politics, and priorities in allocation of the funds in order to meet the research questions raised here. Its concerns were more qualitative than narrowly quantitative.

California and New Jersey were selected as the sample states for one primary reason: to maximize response to the survey. The author had worked for two years as a special assistant to the mayor in Trenton, New Jersey, and had helped form a lobby group of New Jersey mayors.[47] A cover letter to the survey from the mayor carried great weight. Similarly, a cover letter from the director of the Institute for Governmental Studies of the University of California, Berkeley, was expected to give the survey legitimacy in that state. At 83 percent, 86 percent, 91 percent, and 89 percent, the response rates affirmed these hopes.

The study, then, chose to get a detailed look at most of the largest cities in two states rather than a superficial view of many areas. Focusing on cities in two states also allows for more precise analysis. More attention can be paid, for example, to the effect of the specific revenue sources allowed by each state and assignment of expenditure responsibilities among types of government within a state, patterns which vary greatly among the states. Public health may not appear to be an important city priority in a nationwide survey, as in many states it is a county function. Yet in one state it may be very important to cities. Looking at cities in only one state, however, risks having it be a significant outlier. As my late mentor Aaron Wildavsky once told me, data from two states is more than twice as good as data from one.

The two states also provided interesting contrasts. New Jersey, a Northeast industrial state, had been in a period of economic decline through the 1970s and early 1980s; California had continued to prosper. At the time of the first survey, New Jersey had no state income tax, and a larger than average percentage of total revenue was raised by local governments through the property tax; California had a progressive state income tax. Finally, New Jersey was dominated by the strong mayor–weak council form of government; California was reformist. While this two-state sample was not representative in any statistical sense, it was assumed that generalizations about the impact of revenue sharing on large cities could be drawn from it, especially if findings common to the two states overwhelmed the differences in their environment. As it turned out, most of the findings which are used here have been substantiated by both larger national surveys and case studies from other states and individual cities.

THE ANALYSIS EXPANDED—THE PROGRAM ENDS

The termination of the General Revenue Sharing program made it an even more interesting case of intergovernmental aid. Very few programs of this magnitude, with this many governmental beneficiaries and having been enacted with such enthusiasm, face this fate. Why General Revenue Sharing? It would be too simple to blame its death on the drive to reduce the federal budget deficit; after all, many other programs survived and even grew. The revenue sharing story offers lessons about the difficulty of enacting and sustaining sound intergovernmental aid policy, and provides a tour of the rise and fall of the state and local lobby. The fact that states have increasingly shared their revenues with local governments, that other nations continue similar programs, and that Washington continues to debate and pass programs with remarkably similar intent, suggests the inherent soundness of revenue sharing from an intergovernmental policy point of view. This book will pursue these themes.

The Difficulties of Intergovernmental Policy

Public policy is often weakened when theories are of necessity filtered through political processes. This is particularly true of intergovernmental policy in a federal system of government, where inherent fiscal disparities among states justify equalizing grants but any program which targets federal aid based on need results in a loss of political consensus.

The benefits of a program like revenue sharing are easily identifiable for each state, producing relative winners and losers. Formulas make political consensus-building difficult, and the more redistributive, the more difficult it is to build a coalition. The catch-22 of a program like revenue sharing is that if it had been born as a seriously targeted program, one aiding the neediest of subnational governments, it would in all likelihood still be easily justifiable today. However, it most likely would never have won passage in the first place. The redistribution argument is necessary but not sufficient.

The General Revenue Sharing program's enactment and recision suggests the lack of communication between officials at different levels of government, or perhaps at least selective hearing. The analysis here will show that city officials had very different expectations as to the program's impact than did its sponsors in Washington. This gulf was most likely widened by the necessity of selling a program to those unsure of its merits and to the public at large, raising expectations beyond what any honest and informed analysis would have yielded. The problem of proper evaluation, and hence justification for continuance, is compounded by hyperbole and goals made ambiguous to gain political support.

Intergovernmental policy is also sometimes doomed to failure because what is politically rational at the recipient level of government may not always produce results which are rational from the donor's point of view. City officials could be perfectly cautious in the use of revenue sharing funds, acting in not only a politically safe but sound policy manner, and still have the results not produce the political credit the donor expects, however ironic in a program aimed at local discretion. Or local officials under certain circumstances may budget federal funds in such a way as to send a message to Washington, and *not* act in the short-term best interest of program beneficiaries, but hope that such action will produce long-run budgetary gains. Both scenarios are found in the local use of General Revenue Sharing funds. In a federal system, as it should be, doing the right thing from the local perspective may not be the same as doing the right thing from the federal perspective. This dynamic can endanger the affected program.

The Rise and Fall of the Intergovernmental Lobby

The birth, life, and death of General Revenue Sharing also parallels to a great extent the rise and fall of the power of the state and local government lobby in Washington, and particularly those organizations representing cities. By 1972, the year of revenue sharing's passage, cities were already benefiting from Great Society programs targeted to special groups and particular needs. The fact that state and local officials could get Congress to share revenue it raised through taxation, to be used in basically any manner state and local governments desired, was viewed by many at the time as extraordinary. For many local governments the effort to gain enactment of GRS was their first, and for some their last, involvement in the congressional lobbying process. Success was theirs.

However, when you add the difficulty of getting agreement between state officials and local officials to the difficulty of gaining consensus among states and among local governments, you create for program opponents the opportunity for division and then defeat. Consensus breaking is also made easier by the fact that state and local governments have differing business cycles, with one sector often more fiscally flush than the other. Concern for the deficit looms as the final argument for termination of General Revenue Sharing, but other programs, less easily justified, have survived, suggesting a loss of position by the intergovernmental lobby compared to other groups.

In a broader sense, it can be argued that General Revenue Sharing's passage ultimately set the stage for the eventual decline in the types of programs which had been targeted to central city governments under the Great Society. The arguments made to justify the move from categorical to unrestricted aid also ironically may have sown the seeds for revenue sharing's own demise. It took anti-Washington rhetoric to gain support for revenue sharing; that rhetoric took on a life of its own, making it easier for the public to accept a reduction in Washington spending, including General Revenue Sharing. The rhetoric is alive and well in the devolution paradigm of the mid-1990s. Nixon's proclaimed "new American Revolution" has happened—it just took longer than he expected.[48] General Revenue Sharing may have been this revolution's midwife, a short-run sweetener for a long-term shift in governmental responsibility.

The Staying Power of the Revenue-Sharing Idea

While the federal program has come and gone, the sharing of revenue in many different forms and for a variety of reasons continues to grow at the state level. The fact that local governments remain very strongly dependent on the generosity of their state governments suggests that revenue sharing is not such a bad policy idea. Indeed, one could argue that in a truly federal system the national government should learn from the states. The federal government is still theoretically in a better position to raise revenue and redistribute it more equitably than are states. Other nations, notably Canada, have hung on to the concept.

The fiscal problems of many cities, particularly older central cities, may have gotten better in the aggregate, but better is not necessarily good and the aggregate is not all. This book will consider the potential, both policy and political, of a revival of a revenue-sharing-like program, offering recommendations which result from consideration of and modifications to theoretical perspectives which the revenue sharing experience offers. While this suggestion may seem implausible to those who equate federal budget deficits with lack of fiscal ability, one does not have to look too far to find federal government programs, like the Crime Bill, which are not so dissimilar from General Revenue Sharing.

The next chapter offers a more specific and somewhat detailed history of the passage of General Revenue Sharing. Chapter 3 makes use of the survey data and other studies to discuss and analyze city dynamics and decision making regarding the program. Chapter 4 then discusses program termination, while Chapter 5 puts the history of this program in perspective.

NOTES

1. Richard L. Cole, Carl Stenberg, and Carol Weissart, "Two Decades of Change: A Ranking of Key Issues Affecting Intergovernmental Relations," *Publius: The Journal of Federalism* 13 (Fall 1983): 113–122.

2. U.S. Advisory Commission on Intergovernmental Relations, *Significant Features of Fiscal Federalism, vol. 2* (Washington, DC: Advisory Commission on Intergovernmental Relations, December 1994), table C, p. 9.

3. Calculated from U.S. Department of Commerce, Bureau of the Census, *1982 Census of Governments*, vol. 6, number 4 (Washington, DC: U.S. Government Printing Office, 1985): 38.

4. Don Haider, *When Governments Come to Washington* (New York: The Free Press, 1974).

5. See Frances Fox Piven and Richard A. Cloward, *Regulating the Poor: The Functions of Public Welfare* (New York: Vintage Books, 1971).

6. Advisory Commission on Intergovernmental Relations, *Revenue Sharing—An Idea Whose Time Has Come* (Washington, DC: U.S. Government Printing Office, 1970), p. 21.

7. On this point, see Michael D. Reagan and John Sanzone, *The New Federalism* (New York: Oxford University Press, 1972).

8. Deil Wright, *Understanding Intergovernmental Relations* (North Scituate, MA: Duxbury Press, 1978), p. 130.

9. "The State of the Union Message," January 22, 1971, *Weekly Compilation of Presidential Documents* (Washington, DC: Office of the Federal Register, January 25, 1971), p. 93.

10. U.S. Department of Treasury, Office of Revenue Sharing, *Revenue Sharing 1972–1986: A Plain Language Explanation of the Revenue Sharing Program* (Washington, DC: Office of Revenue Sharing, April 1985), p. 5.

11. For an elaboration on this distinction, see Martin Landau, "On the Concept of a Self-Correcting Organization," *Public Administration Review* 33 (1973), 553–547.

12. Patrick Larkey, *Evaluating Public Programs: The Impact of General Revenue Sharing on Municipal Government* (Princeton: Princeton University Press, 1979).

13. John P. Crecine, *Government Problem Solving: A Computer Simulation of Municipal Budgeting* (Chicago: Rand McNally, 1969). See also Arnold J. Meltsner and Aaron Wildavsky, "Leave City Budgeting Alone! A Survey, Case Study, and Recommendations for Reform," in John P. Crecine (ed.), *Financing the Metropolis: Public Policy in Urban Economies* (Beverly Hills, CA: Sage Publications, 1970).

14. For the economics perspective, see Wallace Oates, *Fiscal Federalism* (New York: Harcourt Brace, 1972), and George F. Break, *Financing Government in a Federal System* (Washington, DC: Brookings Institution, 1980). Good discus-

sions of the politics of intergovernmental aid can be found in Jeffrey Pressman, *Federal Programs and City Politics* (Berkeley: University of California Press, 1975), and Deil Wright, *Understanding Intergovernmental Relations*.

15. Aaron Wildavsky, *The Politics of the Budgetary Process* (Boston: Little, Brown and Co., 1964), Chapter Two.

16. For an excellent discussion of the incentives for bureaus and bureaucrats to expand, see Anthony Downs, *Inside Bureaucracy* (Boston: Little, Brown and Co., 1967).

17. Aaron Wildavsky, *Budgeting: A Comparative Analysis* (Boston: Little, Brown and Co., 1975), Chapter Eight.

18. Arnold Meltsner, *The Politics of City Revenue* (Berkeley: University of California Press, 1971), pp. 58–62.

19. Larkey, *Evaluating Public Programs*, p. 97.

20. Arnold Meltsner and Aaron Wildavsky, "Leave City Budgeting," p. 322. For a comprehensive attempt to achieve such a breakdown, see Frank Levy, Arnold Meltsner, and Aaron Wildavsky, *Urban Outcomes: Schools, Streets, and Libraries* (Berkeley: University of California Press, 1974).

21. Aaron Wildvasky, *The Politics of the Budgetary Process*.

22. On satisficing behavior and incrementalism, see, respectively, H.A. Simon, *Administrative Behavior* (New York: Macmillan Company, 1957) and C.E. Lindblom, "The Science of Muddling Through," *Public Administration Review* 19 (1959) pp. 79–88.

23. John P. Crecine, *Government Problem Solving*, p. 235.

24. See Larkey, *Evaluating Public Programs*.

25. Arnold Meltsner and Aaron Wildavsky, "Leave City Budgeting," p. 325.

26. See the annual surveys conducted by the U.S. Advisory Commission on Intergovernmental Relations, *Changing Public Attitudes on Governments and Taxes* (Washington, DC: U.S. Government Printing Office, 1979–1993).

27. Arnold Meltsner and Aaron Wildavsky, "Leave City Budgeting," p. 326.

28. See David O. Sears and Jack Citrin, *The Tax Revolt: Something for Nothing in California* (Cambridge: Harvard University Press, 1985).

29. On the use of microeconomic theory to predict city budget behavior, see, for example, Selma Mushkin and John F. Cotton, *Sharing Funds for State and Local Needs* (New York: Praeger, 1969); Oates, *Fiscal Federalism*; Break, *Financing Government*; and Martin McGuire, "Notes on Grants-in-Aid and Economic Interaction Among Grants," *Canadian Journal of Economics* 6 (1973), pp. 207–221.

30. Patrick Larkey, *Evaluating Public Programs*, p. 71.

31. For a critique of the theory, see Patrick Larkey, *Evaluating Public Programs*, pp. 70–75; also Break, *Financing Government*, pp. 89–101, and Oates, *Fiscal Federalism*, p. 105.

32. Ray Whitman and Robert Cline, "Fiscal Impact of Revenue Sharing," working paper, The Urban Institute, June 1978, p. I–3.

33. It should be noted, however, that even with matching grants economists predict some substitution will occur—that not *all* of the grant will be spent on the designated good.

34. Edward M. Gramlich, "Intergovernmental Grants: A Review of the Empirical Literature," in Wallace E. Oates, ed., *The Political Economy of Fiscal Federalism* (Lexington: Lexington Books, 1977), pp. 229–231.

35. See William Anderson, "Aims, Advantages and Disadvantages, and Consequences," in *Intergovernmental Relations in Review*, 1960, pp. 35–49.

36. Robert Dahl, *Who Governs* (New Haven: Yale University Press, 1961).

37. Wright, *Understanding Intergovernmental Relations*, p. 129.

38. Pressman, *Federal Programs*, p. 133.

39. Pressman, *Federal Programs*, pp. 14–16.

40. James D. Thompson, *Organizations in Action* (New York: McGraw Hill, 1967), pp. 20–21 and p. 35.

41. Jeffrey Pressman, "Political Implications of New Federalism," in Wallace E. Oates, ed., *Financing the New Federalism: Revenue Sharing, Conditional Grants, and Taxation* (Baltimore: Johns Hopkins University Press, 1975), p. 38.

42. Detailed interviews were conducted with four participants (department head, council member, business administrator, mayor) in five New Jersey cities; informal interviews were conducted with various California municipal officials during an annual meeting of the California League of Cities.

43. Catherine Lovell, "Measuring the Effects of General Revenue Sharing: Some Alternative Strategies Applied to 97 Cities," in *Revenue Sharing: Methodological Approaches and Problems*, edited by David A. Caputo and Richard L. Cole (Lexington, MA; Lexington Books, 1976), p. 65.

44. For a more detailed discussion of the methodological issues, see Larkey, *Evaluating Public Programs*, pp. 24–28.

45. Bruce Wallin, book review of *Evaluating Public Programs*, by Patrick Larkey, *Policy Sciences* 13 (1981).

46. Whitman and Cline, "The Fiscal Impact," p. II–3.

47. My experience in Trenton will no doubt inform the analysis at various points.

48. For an excellent elaboration of this point, see Leonard Robins, "The Plot That Succeeded: The New Federalism as Policy Realignment," *Presidential Studies Quarterly* 10, Winter 1980.

2

The Politics of Passage:
An Idea Whose Time Had Come,
and Whose Timing Was Right

The passage of General Revenue Sharing, a program of unrestricted aid to state and local governments, was seen as an anomaly. It did not provide the direct political benefit to members of Congress which categorical grants did, and it even bypassed normal appropriations channels. In providing the "pleasure of spending without the pain of taxation," it seemed altruistic; therefore it surprised some observers of the intergovernmental scene at the time of its passage and others upon later reflection. Yet it had been strongly considered by a Democratic president, introduced by a Republican, and passed by a Democratic Congress, albeit after having been hotly debated with, as in most deliberations of major policy, many subplots at work.

To better understand the many forces which led to its passage, as well as the role it was expected to play, General Revenue Sharing must first be placed in historical context.

FEDERALISM AND THE FOUNDERS

The federal grant-in-aid system at any particular point is the product of many forces, including fiscal position and political initiative. But the Constitution provides the basic structure and ideological guidelines which have shaped the development of the federal role to an extent probably greater than that ever anticipated by the more narrowly pragmatic-minded founders. While the growth of that role has been a result of judicial, political, and fiscal dynamics, sometimes in response to major crises in our nation's history, the fine-tuning of the federal aid system also reflects the influence of charter ideological considerations on changing political motivations.

For purposes of understanding the development of the federal aid system, the most important considerations to emerge from the constitutional convention were philosophical, with some, albeit little, fleshing out in the resulting document itself.[1] The authors of the Constitution were chiefly driven by two events in their recent past: a despotic rule by the British monarchy and the shortcomings of their own first post-Revolution attempt at self-government, the Articles of Confederation. Their overarching, nearly obsessive goal was order—economic, social, and political. The conflict between a desire for limited governmental power and yet the need for an administratively workable form of government is evident throughout the debates. It greatly influenced the form of government ultimately adopted.

The failure of the Articles had produced a cry for a strengthened national (central) government, one which could preserve domestic order and resolve conflicts between the states as well as effectively represent the nation to foreign governments. These administrative concerns were bolstered by the philosophical argument, best put forward by Madison, that a national government would help preserve democracy, especially by preventing the violation of minority rights. He argued that expanding the range of interests would reduce the likelihood that harm would result from the selfish intentions of political factions. Yet the fear of abuse of power by a central government called for balance, and the founders felt that empowered state governments would provide such a check. These arguments, coupled with the obvious political necessity of retaining the states (who were, after all, the original governments) helped produce the federal system of power sharing which came to characterize the United States, a form of government "neither wholly federal nor wholly national."[2] While some feared the ultimate power of the central government and others worried about the militia-backed strength of the states, all could agree at the time on the need to balance and thus hopefully limit the power of government generally.

As with most political documents, the Constitution which won agreement lacked specificity as to how this division of power would be made. The explicit powers of the national government enumerated in Article I Section 8 of the Constitution granted the central government some very important functions, including the regulation of commerce and the conduct of national defense and foreign policy. There were shared powers as well, such as the power to tax and spend. But little was said of specific state responsibilities, other than those relating to their role in elections and in ratifying and amending the Constitution.

For some state advocates this situation was thought to be remedied by the 10th Amendment to the Constitution, ratified in 1791, which perhaps too simply stated "The powers not delegated to the United States by the Constitution, nor prohibited by it to the States, are reserved to the States respectively, or to the people."[3] Interestingly, there had been debate on the floor of the Congress over whether the modifier "explicitly" should be placed before "delegated." It was determined to be unnecessary, an omission which would come back to haunt those favoring states' rights.[4]

GROWTH OF THE FEDERAL GOVERNMENT ROLE

The domestic role of the national government in the federal system was, as we know, to greatly expand in the 200 years following ratification of the Constitution. A report by the U.S. Advisory Commission on Intergovernmental Relations characterizes that growth as the result of "collapsing constraints"—constitutional, political, and fiscal.[5]

Before the 1930s and excluding the Civil War, the most important decisions on the power of the national government versus the states took place in the courts, resulting in a relaxation of the limitations some had thought the Constitution guaranteed. While many Supreme Court decisions are relevant, there is none more important than the 1819 case of *McCulloch* v. *Maryland*.[6] In his decision, Chief Justice John Marshall vastly expanded the potential realm of the national government by broadly interpreting the final clause of Article I, Section 8 of the Constitution, the "necessary and proper" clause. He stated:

> Let the end be legitimate, let it be within the scope of the Constitution, and all means which are appropriate, which are not prohibited, but consistent with the letter and spirit of the Constitution, are Constitutional.[7]

What came to be known as the doctrine of implied powers struck the first blow to the theory of dual federalism, the notion that the national and state governments held distinctive and separate responsibilities, as suggested by the Constitution. In subsequent cases, Supreme Courts broadened the federal role through expanded definitions of commerce (and Congress' ability to regulate it) to include interstate activities which affected it. The court finally ruled during the New Deal that Congress could indeed regulate intrastate activities, rejecting the 10th Amendment as "but a truism."[8]

The assertion of national supremacy was clearly at stake during the Civil War, when southern states considered the Constitution a "compact" which they could break at any time. Might made right, and the victory of the North reconfirmed the notion that the United States was a government of people, not states, and that the national government existed to protect the rights of the individual.

The most formidable breakdown in political constraints on, and public opposition to, an increased federal role occurred during the Great Depression. The nation had been founded on the principle of a negative liberal state, one which above all sought to protect and promote individual liberty, including freedom from government intervention. The inability of many states and unwillingness of others to respond to the economic disaster pushed added responsibilities onto the national government. President Franklin Delano Roosevelt eased this transition, his charismatic leadership combined with the need for some level of government to do something reducing public opposition to new national government intrusions. The pragmatic call for a central government response was not unlike arguments made on behalf of increased national power during the founding debates. This left the American public and its representatives with a curious ambivalence— in favor of specific governmental actions, but still believing in individual initiative; ideologically conservative, yet operationally liberal.[9] Future crises, including the racial strife and urban unrest of the 1950s and 1960s, would again justify increased federal government involvement in areas traditionally viewed as the province of state and local governments.

The third constraint on an increased role for the national government was fiscal: the revenue-raising ability of the national government had been seriously restricted by the Constitution. Even if greater national government intervention was allowed by the courts and accepted by the populace, how could Washington afford it?

The passage of the 16th Amendment and subsequent enactment of an income tax in 1913 put in place the primary mechanism for federal government financing of its added responsibilities, then and in the future.[10] The importance of crises played a role here, too. Increased rates and broader coverage to fund World War I, and the adoption of tax withholding during World War II, made revenue raising easier for Washington.

With less concern for taxpayer flight than states, the federal government could enact a progressive tax structure, with many tax brackets for higher income earners. During inflationary times such as the 1960s and 1970s, this produced revenue increases for the national government greater than increases in the cost of living. Taxpayers were pushed into higher tax brackets, giving birth to the concept of "taxflation." These characteristics, along with the obviously broader tax base, gave the national government great revenue superiority over the states. When tax revenue was inadequate, Washington could also resort to deficit financing, a "luxury" not available to state and local governments.

Constitutional, political, and fiscal obstacles to an increased federal role had to a great extent been overcome by the 1930s. Yet ideological opposition to national government presence in states and communities remained, and it influenced the shape federal programs were to take. Another compromise was in order to balance the liberal–conservative duality of American thought, and the use of grants-in-aid presented the perfect mechanism. The national government could determine priorities and fund activities, but the use of the grant strategy allowed state and local administrators to carry out the bulk of the work, thus reducing potential opposition to what could have been viewed as Washington's encroachments on state and local autonomy.

THE GRANT-IN-AID SYSTEM

Grants are "money payments furnished by a higher to a lower level of government to be used for specified purposes and subject to conditions spelled out in law or administrative regulation."[11] The following brief history of the development of the U.S. grant system highlights the predominant characteristics it was to acquire and sets the stage for an understanding of the criticisms which were to lead to the call for revenue sharing.

The first grants made by the national government were not "money payments" at all, but involved 18th- and 19th-century transfers of federally owned land to state governments, mostly for public education purposes.[12] During this period, the federal government gave away about 15 percent of its landholding to states, the first coming under the Land Ordinance of 1785, and the most notable being the Northwest Ordinance of 1787. Federal largesse was substantially expanded in 1862 with the passage of the first Morrill Land Grant Act, which gave 36,000 acres per member of Congress to each state, a program expanded under 1890's second Morrill Act. The acts required that the land itself, as well as the proceeds from any sale or use thereof, was to be used exclusively for agricultural and mechanical colleges. By the addition of these conditions to the use of the grant, these acts became "the prototype of many current grants."[13]

By 1915, total outlays by the federal government for grant programs had not yet surpassed five million dollars in any year. The federal income tax enabled Washington to become much more generous. Between 1918 and 1930, federal grant program expenditures jumped twentyfold.

Perhaps the most important act passed in the early part of the century was the Federal Aid Highway Act of 1916, which mandated cooperation between the secretary of agriculture and state highway agencies in the building of rural roadways. Two important precedents were set with this act. First, a formula substantively related to the project's goals was developed: funds were allocated to states on the basis of area, population, and rural delivery and star route mileage. Second, the highway program was the first to involve careful supervision of state actions by the donor federal government. "States were required to have proposed projects examined in advance, were required to furnish detailed progress reports, and were subject to audits of expenditures."[14] Red tape had been born.

Along with aid for vocational education, the highway act and grants for agricultural and mechanical education dominated the federal role until the 1930s. During this earlier period another milestone in grant history occurred, the Supreme Court cases of *Massachusetts* v. *Mellon* and *Frothingham* v. *Mellon*.[15] The cases, which involved a small grant program for maternal and child health purposes, were brought to the court separately by an individual citizen and the Commonwealth of Massachusetts. Rejecting the taxpayer's suit, the Supreme Court agreed to rule on Massachusetts' claim that the conditions of the grant program violated the 10th Amendment. In deciding that they did not, the Supreme Court established a principle that has continued to be extremely important today—that no state is *required* to accept any grant; therefore, by volunteering to participate, it forfeits its right to claim interference.[16] The grant is in effect a contract freely entered into by the recipient government.

The next major change in the grant system came during the New Deal of President Roosevelt. For the first time, federal aid programs sought to stimulate employment, better regulate the performance of the economy, and generally provide for the economic security of Americans. It is the shape some of these programs took, however, which is most important. The unemployment compensation program, for example, required that participating states raise revenue by taxing employer payrolls and establish an administrative agency to disburse the funds to unemployed workers. The federal government thus began to demand more from the states for their participation in certain grant programs. Another important precedent set in the New Deal era was the bypassing of state governments by a federal aid program. The Warner–Steagall Act of 1937 made loans and later grants directly to local housing authorities to provide low-rent housing.

During World War II, grant growth slowed, only to rebound at the war's end. Led by programs aimed at education, public health, housing, and transportation, federal aid grew from $2.2 billion in 1950 to $7 billion in 1960. A heightened public awareness of urban poverty, continued civil rights violations in the South, and the death of John F. Kennedy and his succession by a man unsurpassed in his familiarity with the workings of Congress all combined to give Lyndon Johnson's Great Society programs congressional victories, pushing total federal aid to $24 billion by 1970.[17] Aimed primarily at metropolitan areas and disadvantaged populations, the Great Society package included programs such as Model Cities, Community Action Programs, Medicaid, Title I of the Elementary and Secondary Education Act (compensatory education for the disadvantaged), Food Stamps, and housing rehabilitation loans.

The election of a Republican president in 1968 was expected to throw a damper on this trend of unyielding growth. Yet a new dynamic was now at work, one which has been characterized by political scientist Aaron Wildavsky as "Policy as its own Cause."[18] The statutory trap of open-ended programs, along with the political incentive of relevant bureaucracies, congressional committees, and special interests (including those representing state and local governments) to expand program spending pushed the level of grant-in-aid expenditures to new heights. Federal aid spending nearly *doubled* in nominal terms between 1968 and 1972, growing from $18.6 billion to $34.4 billion, and from 10.4 percent of all federal outlays to 14.9 percent.[19] It grew 22.4 percent between 1971 and 1972 alone. The large dollar increases during the 1970s were "chiefly in existing grant programs."[20]

The grant system which existed in the early 1970s involved for the most part grants for designated purposes, and it included requirements for strict supervision by the federal government. These characteristics are indicative of categorical grants—grants which "require that federal funds be expended for specified purposes only and have quite specific planning, record-keeping, and reporting requirements as well."[21] The following provisions are typical of categorical grants:

> statements of permitted uses of funds (such as specifying by law how the funds are to be used or requiring the grantee to submit detailed plans of how the funds are to be used); expenditure constraints (such as that the money 'supplement, not supplant' local funds); requirements that the grantee match the federal contribution with own-source funds; record-keeping and reporting requirements (for example, that grantees maintain accounting records of how they spent federal money); and requirements that nonaccounting data be supplied (such as reports on planned and actual resource use). Most categorical grant programs require the preparation of state or local plans as a condition of receiving aid, and most also require reports of program activities and accomplishments.[22]

Clearly, while providing state and local governments with new revenue, categorical grants do not come free.

The predominance of categorical grants in the federal aid system was beyond dispute, and the preference of Congress for categorical grants was the result of many forces. Congress likes the categorical approach chiefly because it allows members to take credit for the programs which result. Members love being able to appear at ribbon-cutting ceremonies opening, for example, a new park financed by federal funds. The connection is direct, and is one which the member hopes his or her constituents will recall at election time. Further, internal congressional norms suggest that the more dollars and programs a committee or subcommittee supervises, the more important that committee is. Thus the specialization of the grant system neatly matches the specialization of Congress. Categorical grants also allow the targeting of federal money to specific groups who are deemed deserving by Congress. Finally, tight controls on the use of federal money acts to mollify the concerns of fiscal conservatives who fear misuse of the funds at the state and local level. It is not surprising, therefore, that before 1966 nearly all federal grant programs were categorical in nature, and that as late as 1970 categorical grants accounted for 95 percent of federal grant-in-aid money.[23]

Criticisms of categorical grants began to mount by the late 1960s, however. Critics, particularly recipient governments, saw categorical grant programs as too restrictive, not flexible enough to allow for tailoring and adaptation to city or state specific conditions. Further, there was duplication and overlap among some grant programs, while a proliferation of grants at work in a similar geographic area, yet administered by different federal agencies, made coordination difficult. Block grant programs, the second major type of aid to emerge, first appeared in 1966 and were a response to these concerns.

The characteristics of block grants are as follows:

1. Recipient jurisdictions have fairly wide discretion within the designated program or functional area.
2. Administration, reporting, planning, and other program features are intended to keep grantor supervision and control at a minimum.
3. Formula-based allocation provisions are intended to limit grantor discretion and decrease fiscal uncertainty for the grantees.
4. Eligibility provisions are fairly precise, tending to favor general as opposed to special district governments, retaining grantor administrative discretion, and favoring state and local generalist officials over program specialists.
5. Funding provisions tend toward specifying low matching requirements for recipient jurisdictions.[24]

Block grants, then, designate broad goals and leave the means to these ends to local discretion to a much greater extent than do categorical grants. The first block grant program was the Partnership for Health Act, followed closely by the Safe Streets Act of 1968. Block grants grew from $0.3 billion in 1970 to $5.4 billion in 1975, and from 5 to 11 percent of the federal grant-in-aid budget.

GENERAL REVENUE SHARING

An even more radical departure from the existing federal grant system, also in response to the perceived shortcomings of categorical grants, came with the enactment of the General Revenue Sharing program in 1972.

Revenue Sharing in History

The concept of revenue sharing goes back to the earliest days of the republic. Thomas Jefferson's second inaugural address recognized the possible dilemma of national government income in excess of needs and suggested that federal revenues in such an instance be used for "... a just repartition among the states ... applied to rivers, canals, roads, ports, manufacturers, education, and other great objects within each state."[25] By the 1830s, revenue did indeed exceed expenditures. At the same time, states were spending heavily on internal improvements and public works, and were pressed to finance these needs.

A proposal was made in Congress to distribute federal surpluses when they existed, and in 1836 Congress passed the first revenue sharing bill:

> The Distribution Act of 1836 had many peculiar features. It provided for apportionment among the states, according to their federal representation and in four quarterly installments, of the surplus revenue in the Treasury on January 1, 1837. But since outright distribution might bring a Presidential veto, the sums were explicitly declared to be on deposit and the Secretary of the Treasury was given certificates which the states were to be obligated to meet if the Treasury was in need of funds. It was an open secret that all of this was a false front, and yet President Jackson glossed over his reluctance to sign the bill by pretending that deposits were genuine and by asserting that to use them as gifts would be a "violation of public faith and moral obligation."[26]

The initial amount authorized for distribution was $37.5 million. About $28 million was actually distributed in 1837 and was used for a variety of purposes by the states. Some of it went to state banking systems, some toward paying off local debt, and some for public works. The greater part of the distribution, however, was given to education.

Not everyone viewed the program as a success. Historian Edward Bourne found the results disastrous, concluding:

> ... that distribution of the surplus of 1837 helped plunge the country into a financial crisis; that money was squandered on canals, railroads, and other internal improvements that were never finished or could never pay for themselves, and that the windfall was demoralizing to the people because it got them out of the habit of paying taxes just when they were getting deeply into debt.[27]

The depression that hit the nation during this period further highlighted an emerging problem of fiscal federalism:

> The history of the period throws light upon the fiscal problem of federalism, since it gives a clear example of a maladjustment of governmental functions and resources. The federal government, because of constitutional restrictions and still more because of the political pattern, had a range of functions more limited than its fiscal resources; the states had undertaken duties which were more extensive than they could finance.[28]

The parallels between that era and the conditions of the late 1960s and early 1970s are noteworthy.

The more direct line of revenue sharing ancestry can be traced to the late 1940s, when the concept reemerged. In 1949 Representative E.P. Scrivner of Kansas introduced H.R. 1582 in the 80th Congress. It was to authorize the Internal Revenue Service to transfer to state treasuries, on a quarterly basis, 1 percent of the federal individual and corporate income tax collected within the states. The revenues were to be used for "educational purposes only, without any federal direction, control, or interference."[29] It was never given serious consideration by the Congress.

Modern Revenue Sharing: The Executive Branch

While there were other unsuccessful proposals made in Congress in the intervening years, the immediate line of ancestry of the ultimately successful effort of 1972 begins in the executive branch and dates back to a task force appointed in 1964 by President Johnson. Headed by Joseph Pechman, its final report borrowed heavily from ideas developed earlier by the chairman of the Council of Economic Advisors, Walter Heller, and thus came to be known as the Heller–Pechman proposal.

An economic boom had produced a surplus in the federal treasury reminiscent of the 1830s, and "Heller suggested revenue sharing as the instrument that would simultaneously help eliminate part of the fiscal drag of expected annual federal revenue surpluses and build up the fiscal strength of state and local governments."[30] One plan would have distributed 2 percent of the federal income tax base to states and localities, primarily on a per capita basis.

Johnson also was said to favor the program based on the need to remedy both horizontal and vertical fiscal imbalance. Horizontal fiscal imbalance refers to the fact that some states and some local governments are poorer than others, and thus it is more difficult for them to raise the revenue necessary to adequately fund services. Johnson felt that this rationale could gain him support among the liberals in Congress. Vertical fiscal imbalance suggests that while it is easier for the national government to raise revenue, due to its broader base and limited fear of tax competition, state and local governments are in a better position to identify citizen needs and tailor responses to them. This imbalance between revenue-raising ability and determination of spending needs could be remedied by unrestricted federal aid. The president thought this rationale would win over congressional conservatives who were afraid that states were losing power in the federal system.

The proposal never made it to Congress, however. One of the reasons why is a classic case of timing and politics. John Shannon, who was at the U.S. Advisory Commission on Intergovernmental Relations at the time and working on revenue sharing, remembers Walter Heller telling him that he had gone to brief President Johnson on the program and was kept waiting in the lobby of the White House for hours.[31] The president was apparently occupied with a breaking scandal involving one of his aides, Walter Jenkins. Heller never got to brief the president, but a story about revenue sharing had been leaked to the *New York Times*. Labor leader George Meaney immediately called the president "to raise hell," arguing there were better ways to spend the money. Upset at the leak and the response, LBJ had his aides call to demand that everyone with a copy of the Heller–Pechman report (which were numbered) burn it. According to Shannon, the subject of revenue sharing was *verboten* for the next four or five years, until Nixon.

Had revenue sharing been proposed and enacted under Johnson, its primary rationale—eliminating fiscal drag by giving some of a surplus to state and local governments—would have been very different than the arguments which were eventually successful. While President Johnson may have been gun-shy after his Meaney experience, rising expenditures on the Vietnam War, various tax cuts, and the rising costs of the Great Society programs more than disposed of the brief federal budget surplus.[32]

At a time when electoral support of state and local officials was still important, both party platforms in the 1968 presidential campaign endorsed a program of revenue sharing. The winner, Richard Nixon, viewed with typical Republican dismay the growth in the number of categorical grant programs from fewer than 200 to over 1,000 in the previous decade, a trend toward complexity, and a concentration of power in the nation's capital that had been characteristic of the grant system throughout its history. His response was to offer a program:

> . . . moving away from the current strong reliance on particularistic and highly structured federal grant-in-aid instruments and emphasizing instead new approaches which seek to strengthen the political structure and enhance the responsiveness of American federalism.[33]

His approach would include a program of revenue sharing. In a nationwide television address on August 8, 1969, Nixon outlined his philosophy:

> For a third of a century, power and responsibility have flowed toward Washington—and Washington has taken for its own the best sources of revenue.
> We intend to reverse this tide, and to turn back to the States a greater measure of responsibility—not as a way of avoiding problems, but as a better way of solving problems. I shall propose to the Congress next week that a set portion of the revenues, from federal income taxes, be remitted directly to the states—with a minimum of federal restrictions on how those dollars are to be used, and with a requirement that a percentage of them be channeled through for the use of local government.[34]

Revenue sharing was to be a part of what Nixon termed "the New Federalism," the first time that now-oft-repeated name was used.

Of course, there were once again behind-the-scenes subplots. Jim Martin, who was a lobbyist for the National Governors Association, recalls that Vice President Spiro Agnew's ambitions played a role.[35] Finding little to do in his role as vice president, Agnew, a former governor and county commissioner, went to an annual meeting of the Governors Association, which was in Puerto Rico. He asked several of his governor friends if they would tell President Nixon they wanted Agnew to be in charge of intergovernmental relations for the President. When they agreed, Agnew immediately loaded several of them on to Air Force One, along with Martin. They landed at Andrews Air Force Base, where a helicopter and then a limousine whisked them to the White House Office and in to the Oval Office. Upon hearing the request of the governors, Nixon said, "But you're too busy, aren't you Spiro?"

Agnew replied, "I'd love to do it, Mr. President." The vice president soon visited the governors again and asked how he could repay them. The answer? "Give us revenue sharing."

The original Nixon revenue sharing program was presented as a supplement to, not a substitute for, the existing grant system. With a first-year allocation of $500 million expected to rise to $5 billion by fy1976, the program was never taken up by the 91st Congress. Richard Nathan comments, "The small first-year allocation, the designation of states as the agents for the intrastate distribution of funds, and the administration's own concentration on welfare reform may have contributed to the inaction."[36]

That designation of states as the agents for distribution of funds to local governments within their states had kept local officials from throwing their full support behind the Nixon proposal and thus weakened a potentially strong coalition. According to Shannon, the next defining moment for revenue sharing was the birth of that coalition of state and local leaders. At a summit meeting at the U.S. Advisory Commission on Intergovernmental Relations, Art Naftalin, mayor of Minneapolis, took the lead for the mayors' point of view. He argued that while states have many revenue sources at their disposal, local governments were hand-cuffed by state law and the realities of local tax competition. Some governors disagreed. Finally, Nelson Rockefeller, governor of New York, cleared his throat and the room fell silent. "I'm going to say something now that as a governor I shouldn't say," Shannon remembers him saying. "I want federal takeover of welfare more than I want revenue sharing. But since it won't happen, revenue sharing is the next best thing. If we're going to get it, we need a large slice to flow directly to local governments."

"We can stop anything in the Senate," he continued, "but the mayors can stop anything in the House." Shannon recalls thinking at the time that if it had been the governor from South Dakota, he would have been "blown out of the water." But Rockefeller was bigger than life, and from the State of New York. Rockefeller also proposed the ultimately accepted 2/3 local, 1/3 state split of revenue sharing, apparently with no basis other than a desire to gain and motivate local support. Two or three weeks later, Shannon recalls, a group of mayors was invited to a meeting of the Governors Association, the first time that had happened. The desire for the new, unrestricted form of federal aid had allowed state and local leaders to overcome their occasional animosity toward each other.

Aware of the new coalition, and in need of evidence of a concern for domestic problems on the eve of a reelection campaign, Nixon again proposed revenue sharing in his 1971 State of the Union address,

along with six broad-purpose "special revenue sharing" programs
(block grants) for Law Enforcement, Manpower Training, Urban and
Rural Community Development, Transportation, and Education, all
part of what he termed "a new American revolution." In arguing that
state and local government officials, closer to the problems of their
constituency, could better respond to its particular needs, he stated:

> If we put more power in more places, we can make government more
> creative in more places. For that way we multiply the number of people
> with the ability to make things happen—and we can open the way to a
> new burst of creative energy throughout America.[37]

The federal government had been running a consistent deficit, so there
was no need to eliminate any fiscal drag. Nor was the purpose of
the Administration's General Revenue Sharing program necessarily
redistributive or aimed at horizontal inequities, as the Administration's
initial formula for distribution was based solely on the criteria of population and tax effort. It did rely on the vertical imbalance argument,
however, noting that the federal income tax had a greater elasticity
than state and local taxes (predominantly sales and property taxes)—
that is, that revenue from the federal income tax rose faster than national
income, while the other taxes responded in more direct proportion to
it. In the face of rapidly rising state and local expenditures, revenue
sharing was to help ease the burden. President Nixon commented
specifically on the potential use of the funds for much-needed local
property tax relief. Revenue sharing was to be an "investment in renewing state and local government," which could "rescue the states and
localities from the brink of financial crisis."[38]

Nixon's pronouncements on the program relied heavily on anti-
categorical grant, and hence anti-Washington, rhetoric. He often repeated that his goal was to reinvigorate state and local governments
by putting decision making closer to the people. Revenue sharing
would be more administratively efficient than existing grants, and
its use would be more democratically determined. General Revenue
Sharing would "make government more creative and responsive by
shifting power from the federal level closer to the people."[39]

The new plan was sent to Congress in a special message on February 4, 1971, and was introduced on February 9. It proposed sharing
an amount equal to 1.3 percent of total taxable personal income, approximately $5 billion in the first full year. Obviously, that amount would
grow with federal revenues. Distributions would be made to states on
the basis of population, with an adjustment for tax effort, and there
was provision for pass-through to local governments of approximately

half of the states' allocation.[40] The Administration's special revenue sharing block grant proposals involved the consolidation of categorical grant programs totaling $10 billion, and included $1 billion in new money.

There were some who felt that Nixon and Agnew thought all along that Congress would never pass General Revenue Sharing, and that they could thus get the political credit from governors and mayors without the cost. But as the Advisory Commission on Intergovernmental Relations had intoned, revenue sharing was "An Idea Whose Time Has Come."[41]

Congress and Revenue Sharing

Revenue sharing initially met immediate and strong opposition. The story in the *Congressional Quarterly Weekly Report* was entitled "Revenue Sharing: Bitter Battle Looms in Congress."[42] Wilbur Mills (D-ARK), chairman of the powerful House Ways and Means Committee, was viewed at that time as *the* most powerful member of Congress. After a meeting at the White House, Mills said he would certainly hold hearings on the administration's plan, "but not for the purpose of promoting the plan—for the purpose of killing it."[43] How strongly did he feel? "I think this is the most dangerous program ever developed."[44]

His opposition was most directly related to his fiscal conservatism. The federal government was already running a deficit, and he felt it could not afford the largesse. In addition, he and many of his conservative Southern colleagues did not take kindly to the notion of separating taxing and spending responsibility, as revenue sharing would. In speaking of the earlier proposal, Mills had said:

> I have always felt strongly that the level of government that spends money should have the responsibility for raising that amount of money. If we turn back to the states a part of what we in Congress levy and raise, then we have relieved states of a responsibility they should meet themselves.[45]

Holding the position that the tendency to spend among elected officials is insatiable unless checked by the need to raise taxes, Mills predicted that the program would result in an unnecessarily enlarged public sector. Finally, he objected to the distribution of funds. "Why do I say that it is wasteful? Because under any of the formulas that have been developed so far, substantial funds are given to States and localities where there is little or no need. . . ."[46]

Mills found support among other members of Congress, who often had their own reasons for taking this position. Some did not like the linkage of general to special revenue sharing, the latter being seen as a direct threat to the congressional subsystems which revolved around the categorical grants. Others fell prey to the anti-revenue-sharing lobbying of business groups who opposed higher taxes and labor who, fearful that revenue sharing might be used for tax relief, supported the traditional job-stimulating categorical grant approach.[47]

Nevertheless, support for passage was building; over 100 revenue sharing bills were introduced in the 91st Congress.[48] Senator Edmund Muskie (D-ME), who introduced his own plan, argued that revenue sharing would "assist state and local governments in providing services which are best provided by levels of government closest to the people."[49] Joseph Pechman testified:

> Since most state and local taxes are, on balance, regressive (bearing more heavily on low-income persons than high-income persons), rising state and local taxes have imposed unnecessarily harsh burdens on the poor. Revenue sharing is needed to make up for the deficient tax-paying capacity of low-income persons to support non-poverty-related activities of state and local government.
>
> Without such relief, cities will continue to lose middle-income and high-income families, who will neither tolerate the inadequate public services that their poor neighbors must accept nor pay higher taxes to carry the burden for these neighbors. Revenue sharing is not a panacea for all the ills of state and local government. But it would certainly help to strengthen our federal system of government at a time when it needs to be strengthened.[50]

At the same hearings Walter Heller testified that revenue sharing would allow state and local officials the opportunity to "flex their decision-making muscles," muscles which had presumably atrophied from non-use after years of categorical, dictates-attached grants.[51] As Secretary of the Treasury John Connally testified, "The existing federal aid system is fragmented and overcontrolled."[52]

State and local officials weighed in heavily. New York City Mayor John V. Lindsay reminded members of Congress of the limited revenue-raising ability of cities and the negative effects of some federal-aid programs:

> We have asked the state for the power to tax ourselves again to preserve the city. But the state government seems determined to deny us even that small measure of home rule. . . . National policies not only failed to stem the deterioration of the nation's cities, they actually spawned it, nursed it, and raised it to full maturity.[53]

The federal highway program and housing act had been blamed by many for urban flight, and welfare policies were seen as creating dependent populations in central cities. Mayor Ken Gibson of Newark agreed, noting the problems of rampant unemployment, crime, drugs, poverty, decay, and disease, concluding:

> ... these problems are national in scope. And yet we at the local level with the least resources are being asked to provide hope and opportunity to those who would have been left out of the American dream.[54]

At a 1971 meeting of the Legislative Action Committee of the New Jersey Conference of Mayors, Joseph Nardi, the mayor of Camden, painted an easier-to-understand portrait: "I've got a city of 100,000 people, and I have no movie theaters, no grocery stores, and only one drug store left."[55]

A final argument for revenue sharing was in response to a problem that was to linger and grow, prodding Congress to finally pass legislation to check itself: unfunded mandates. George Lehr, county executive of Jackson County, Missouri, spoke for the National Association of Counties and said that revenue sharing was needed to "solve the fiscal problems arising from our willingness to assume the responsibilities accorded to us (and sometimes mandated upon us) by federal and state governments. . . ."[56]

It soon became clear to some observers that the question was no longer whether a bill would pass, but what type. Mills, himself, did an about-face by the end of 1971, responding to the horizontal fiscal imbalance argument that:

> ... the lack of an aggregate fiscal problem conceals the fact that there does exist a severe imbalance between the needs and resources of particular jurisdictions. . . .[57]

Mills and nine other members of the House Ways and Means Committee introduced HR 11950 on November 30, 1971. Mills' shifting of the distribution of funds from a 50–50 state–local split to the 1/3–2/3 division recognized that local governments were the more fiscally pressed, and implicitly accepted the compromise of the state and local coalition.

It was not very difficult to present a gloomy picture of many of the nation's cities. The urban fiscal crisis had resulted from two reenforcing conditions: the poor, increasingly concentrated in the cities, needed special services, and they were unable to contribute substantially to the financing of these government services. The costs, then, were shifted through taxes to middle-income residents, who had to pay a higher price for a lower level of service than some of their suburban neighbors—usually not for long, however, as witnessed by the suburban exodus of the 1960s. Cities soon found themselves caught in a vicious cycle of raising taxes, causing a taxpayer exodus, shrinking the base, and thereby causing still higher tax rates, etc. Commuters benefited from central city services without paying for them.

The Ways and Means Committee report which was eventually to accompany the bill noted:

> In considering the financial problems of local governments, your committee came to the conclusion that many localities face most severe financial crises. . . .
>
> Closely related to this is the problem arising from the limited jurisdictions of many local governments: they often are called upon to provide many services for persons who do not live in their taxing jurisdiction. At the same time, those within their taxpaying jurisdictions often are poor and unable to pay for their share of the services demanded.[58]

As it sought to redress these disparities, the program was intended to be at least somewhat redistributive.

Others argued that the conversion of Mills was more political than intellectual, tied to his brief testing of the presidential waters and consequent need for big-city votes. Those who pursue this line of reasoning offer another substantive switch in the program—Mills' successful drive to add "general tax effort" to the "income tax effort" element of the distribution formula—which in addition to favoring the South would presumably gain the good graces of officials in the non-income-tax state of New Hampshire.[59]

Nearly all analysts of the change in Mills and the program's ultimate passage point to the importance of the effort undertaken by state and local officials on revenue sharing's behalf. Don Haider wrote at the time that, "The enactment of revenue sharing, in effect, marked the high point thus far in joint work of the government interest groups to influence their federal constituency."[60] This study's survey indicated that of eighty-three city chief executives responding to the 1972 survey, sixty-seven said that they had participated in the national lobby effort, and twenty-nine of those sixty-seven noted that they had *never* before participated in a national lobby effort to this extent (Table 2-1). At the annual meeting of the National League of Cities in 1971, a "lobby packet" for General Revenue Sharing was distributed to those in attendance. It included for the first time a "sample letter" to be sent to

---

TABLE 2-1
Number of Cities Surveyed that Took Part in
Lobbying

Participation:		Participated Before:	
None	16	Yes	29
Some	38	No	38
Substantial	29		

---

members of Congress. Congressional staffers reported that some local officials were so unfamiliar with the ins and outs of lobbying that they just signed the sample letter and sent it in.

In the middle of the debate in the Ways and Means Committee, President Nixon reaffirmed his support for revenue sharing in his 1972 State of the Union address:

> Revenue sharing still remains on the list of unfinished business. I call again today for the enactment of revenue sharing . . . the need for revenue sharing becomes more acute as time passes. The financial crisis of state and local governments is deepening. The pattern of breakdown in state and municipal services grows more threatening. Inequitable tax pressures are mounting. The demand for more flexible and more responsive government—at levels closer to the problems and closer to the people—is building.[61]

With the consent of Mills, the Ways and Means Committee reported a bill, HR 14730, on April 26, 1972.

There were seven members of the committee who filed dissenting views, and they nicely summarize most of the objections to revenue sharing, including:

- Divorce of tax-raising responsibility from spending authority.
- Restructuring of federal–state–local relationships.
- Lack of surplus revenues to share.
- Failure of the bill to deal with the existing weaknesses of state and local government.
- Lack of any rationale for the amounts of money or relationship of the amounts to state or local needs.
- Lack of a rationale for the various formulas.
- Failure of the bill to take account of federal aid programs or state aid to local governments.
- Lack of effective accountability requirements.[62]

Some Democrats merely did not wish to support an initiative of a Republican president.

But also extremely important to the opposition, if unmentioned by members of Congress, was the importance of political credit, which would be less direct and obvious under revenue sharing:

> Many in Congress regard supervision of the use of federal funds as their prerogative and responsibility. They take the position that it is their duty to establish the conditions within which a grant of federal money is to be spent. Interwoven with the concept of responsibility is the concept of credit for grants distributed to state and local governments.
>
> Members of Congress expect to gain politically from the distribution of federal funds in their states and districts. Dispensing of funds and benefits to segments of society must be regular and continuous for maximum political effect. The existing aid system provides fresh opportunities continually for distribution of federal largesse. Revenue sharing would be limited in benefits of this type.[63]

The Governors Association's Martin remembers two interesting things about the floor debate as it wound toward a final vote in the House. First, it was the very first time that computer printouts were used to help analyze a bill, allowing each member of Congress to see exactly how his or her district would do under the proposed formulas. This was soon to become commonplace in any debate regarding program initiation, expansion, or cutback, and has made getting agreement much more difficult.

Second, he recalls Congressman Mahon (D-TX), chairman of the Appropriations Committee, which would be bypassed under a revenue sharing program, bringing twelve to fifteen committee and subcommittee chairs to the floor to argue against revenue sharing. In response, the decision was made by supporters to include the previously excluded "places under 2,500 population" in the program. It turned out that this added only 5–8 percent to the cost of the program and won many votes. Ironically, Martin argues, this change produced what later became one of the biggest criticisms of the program, and helped to cause its termination: it went to places that didn't need it and helped to prop up inefficient and unnecessary local governments. The State and Local Fiscal Assistance Act was passed by the House on June 22 by a 274–122 roll call vote.

Providing further indication of the rising importance of revenue sharing, Senate hearings began a week later. After hearing arguments pro and con, similar to those made in the House, the Senate Finance Committee reported its version on August 11 and an amended version on August 16.

The Report of the Senate Finance Committee which eventually accompanied the General Revenue Sharing bill reaffirmed the importance of the urban fiscal problem in its support of the program:

> The financial soundness of our State and local governments is essential to our Federal system. However, the committee's studies have led it to the conclusion that the State and local governments now face financial problems of a most severe nature. Today, it is the States, and even more especially the local governments, which bear the brunt of our more difficult domestic problems. The need for public services has increased manyfold and their costs are soaring. At the same time, State and local governments are having considerable difficulty in raising the revenue necessary to meet these costs.
>
> Moreover, while most State and local governments are experiencing financial difficulties, for many core cities the financial problems are particularly acute. The flight of middle income and high income people to the suburbs has left core cities with the severe fiscal burden of providing services to large numbers of relatively low income people who are able to pay only a relatively small share of the cost of government services.[64]

The only meaningful floor addition to the committee's bill was a prevailing wage requirement. The bill passed the Senate on September 12, 1972, by a 64–20 roll call vote.

The prime area of disagreement between the two versions was the distribution formula: the House version favored urbanized areas, and the Senate bill contained a Southern and rural bias. The conference committee, with an election six weeks away, forged a "highly unusual compromise which allowed each state the larger of the revenue-sharing allocation its state and local governments would receive under the conflicting House- and Senate-approved distribution formulas."[65] They reported the compromise on September 25. The House accepted the report on October 12 with a 265–110 vote, and the Senate voted 59–19 to approve it a day later. On October 20, President Nixon signed the bill into law in Constitution Hall, Philadelphia.

Details of the Program

As initially implemented, the State and Local Assistance Act of 1972 automatically dispersed roughly $6 billion a year to state and local government, the largest domestic aid program ever enacted by Congress.[66] One-third of the funds allocated to a state went to the state government itself, with the remaining two-thirds divided among the general-purpose units of local government. The state government could use its funds in any manner it deemed important, while local governments were required to use the money on "priority expenditures" defined as

1. Ordinary and necessary maintenance and operating expenses for:
    (i) Public safety (including law enforcement, fire protection, and building code enforcement);
    (ii) Environmental protection (including sewage disposal, sanitation, and pollution abatement);
    (iii) Public transportation (including transit systems and streets and roads);
    (iv) Health;
    (v) Recreation;
    (vi) Libraries;
    (vii) Social services for the poor and aged; and
    (viii) Financial administration, and
2. Ordinary and necessary capital expenditures as authorized by law.[67]

Local governments could not use the funds for educational purposes (except for capital improvements under "2"), nor as matching funds for other federal programs. Separate trust funds had to be established to receive the funds, plans and reports on their use were to be submitted to the Treasury Department and published locally, and state and local governments were subject to audit. Antidiscrimination laws applied, and prevailing wage rates were to be paid.

In theory, then, local governments could not use any of their revenue sharing allocation for tax reduction or in areas not deemed high priority. In practice, however, this was not the case. Local governments could shift locally raised funds from any of the high priority areas, replace them with revenue sharing money, and use the "released" funds for whatever purpose they wished, including tax relief.[68] The difficulty in determining exactly how the funds were used is thus apparent, and gives validity to the approach of seeking the uses and impact as perceived by local officials.

Perhaps the most complicated part of the program involved the formulas used to distribute the funds to state and local governments. The total share allocated to a state was that which was the greater result of applying two formulas: the five-factor House formula, based on general population, urbanized population, inverse per capita income, state income tax collection, and the general tax effort of the state; or the Senate formula, based on general population, inverse per capita income, and general tax effort. State governments then took their one-third share. The latter formula (Senate) was subsequently used to allocate shares among county areas within the state, with county governmental units themselves entitled to a share equal to the proportion of their tax levy to those of all governmental units within the county area. The Senate formula was then again used to allocate the remainder to municipal governments, villages, townships, etc.

Two other elements of the program as passed deserve highlighting. First, the program was not revenue sharing in the true sense of apportioning a set percentage of federal revenue. While this was a characteristic of some of the earlier plans and versions, "The bill provides for the distribution of specific dollar amounts of fiscal assistance rather than any percentage of federal revenues. This is a significant difference because it means that the federal government is not adding a new uncontrollable expenditure category."[69] Second,

> this bill provides the fiscal assistance for a limited five-year period. This assures a review of the financial problems of state and local governments after a period of time, with the result that provision can be made for needed changes as they develop. It also gives assurance that these funds will be available to states and localities during the current period when, because of economic and other problems, the need for this assistance may well be at a peak.[70]

Intended to mollify critical fiscal conservatives in Congress, these provisions were to greatly effect the budgetary decisions of local officials. Revenue sharing was reauthorized by Congress in 1976 for three and three-quarters years, in 1980, and in 1983 for local governments only.

A Short Honeymoon

The program, which had faced vociferous criticism during congressional consideration of the program by fiscal conservatives, drew strong fire from the left both during and after deliberation. Liberals sought to answer a troubling question: Why would a Republican president enact a program which was at least mildly targeted to central cities?

Vernon Jordan of the Urban League challenged the "decision-making closer to the people is better" argument, noting "so are the insensitivities and the biases and prejudices of the local government closer to the people and they are closer in a way that they operate, I think, more oppressively. . . ."[71] A *New Republic* editorial had warned:

> The political clout of the urban poor and minorities is rarely powerful enough to compete with that of rural claimants. There are larger

constituencies behind street paving and larger police forces than behind welfare reform or compensatory education.[72]

The editorial went on to argue, "Mr. Nixon has come to realize that the cities, and more recently large industrial states, are starving. He knows that those who starve do not too closely examine the nutritional content of a crust of bread."[73]

Related to these concerns, and a prophetic criticism, was that espoused by a minority of mayors at the National League of Cities meetings of 1969 and 1971. These local officials, accused at the time of looking a gift horse in the mouth, argued that the General Revenue Sharing was not to be supported if it were to ultimately substitute for the categorical aid programs already in place. Those programs, it was offered, were targeted to the special needs of cities, and furthermore served a useful political insulation purpose for many local officials. The majority ruled, however, assured by the Administration that this was not to be the case. The mayors nonetheless announced as a principle that revenue sharing "should augment federal grants, and not merely substitute for such aids."[74]

In the political world, today's assurances too often become tomorrow's broken promises. By January 1973, a postelection President had made economic management his number one goal. Nixon worried about the potential inflationary impact of increased government spending as the economy came out of recession. Don Haider relates:

> With a landslide Presidential victory behind him . . . the President moved on a broad front to eliminate more than a hundred categorical programs, to impose a freeze on federal housing subsidies, and to shut out future applications for a variety of grant programs like water and sewer aid and open space grants. He also persisted in impounding funds previously appropriated by Congress for expenditure.[75]

Business Week magazine noted at the time, "The 1974 budget cuts deep in a great many areas, and such programs as model cities, federally aided hospital construction, and cheap rural electrification loans as well as the Office of Economic Opportunity simply vanish."[76] Some cuts were to be made up by including affected programs in Nixon's special revenue sharing block grant proposals, but the bottom line cuts were still to amount to $6.5 billion in existing programs in fy1973, $16.9 billion in fy1974, and a projected $21.7 billion cut in fy1975.[77]

Haider goes on to argue that the passage of General Revenue Sharing had created a "budgetary gap" that President Nixon wanted to close. He had no qualms about suggesting that the mayors use the new unrestricted aid to substitute for (not, as he had said, to supplement) categorical aid. "The White House . . . repeatedly indicated that the antipoverty program, public service employment, library assistance, and a host of social service programs specified for phaseout or reduction could be continued if states and localities wanted to use their new general revenue sharing funds to do so."[78]

While controlling the growth of federal government expenditures was clearly one of the goals of the President's cutbacks, others could be deduced. From a managerial perspective, it could be argued that many of the Great Society programs had been enacted without standards of evaluation. Faced with the decision to renew or end these programs, the President, through his proposed consolidation of programs into block grants at reduced funding levels, would in effect force state and local officials, closer to the issues, to make the difficult decisions as to which programs were worthy of continuance and which were not.[79] In more partisan terms, the moves reflected (1) the traditional Republican distaste for large-scale social programs and (2) the fact that President Nixon had inherited a huge Democratic bureaucracy in Washington, over which he had little control. Finally, some suggested that "revenue sharing could serve as a device for splitting up the old Democratic coalition, turning minority groups and grant constituencies against mayors who failed to use their revenue sharing funds to support local programs."[80]

The mayors were not pleased. East St. Louis Mayor Williams commented, "General Revenue Sharing is a hoax," a charge echoed by Kansas City Mayor Charles B. Wheeler, Jr.[81] Seattle Mayor Wes Uhlman elaborated:

> I suppose we can say the New Federalism is a great deal like a Trojan horse that has been left to us, not filled with enemy soldiers in this instance, but with broken promises (such as) program freezes and lopsided funding formulae, cynical pretexts and with an executive budget that will spell disaster for American cities. . . .[82]

Mayor Landrieu of New Orleans reminded, "We have never, and will never, view revenue sharing as a substitute for the categoricals."[83] Richard Nathan suggested that these moves would create an undesirable pincer effect for local governments, and Paul Dommel concluded, "Had revenue sharing been offered by the Nixon Administration as the ultimate policy for repealing parts of the New Deal and much of the Great Society, the effort would certainly have failed."[84] The President was attempting to use policy decrementalism and decentralization—some called it a shell game—to accomplish the same ends.

In the short term, the effort failed. Congress, defending its preference for categorical grants, rejected most of the cuts. Speaker Carl
Albert noted that we "will not permit the President to lay waste the
great programs . . . which we have developed during the decades
past."[85] While the only major reduction in categorical funding to occur
was in the Model Cities program, fear and uncertainty had been injected
into the budgetary calculations of mayors across the land. They remained adamant in their opinion that revenue sharing funds would
not be used to substitute for what they viewed as federal responsibilities. And while the Nixon Administration attempt to cut back on social
programs may have failed in the short run, the anti-Washington rhetoric
it took to pass revenue sharing spread, helping to set the stage for the
neoconservative movement, the "Tax Revolt," and ultimately a great
scaling back of federal government aid to cities.

SUMMARY

Many forces have to converge for major legislation to be enacted,
including program rationale, political motivation, and availability of
financial resources.

General Revenue Sharing provided more than enough varied rationales to garner congressional support. The initial argument of the fiscal
drag of a surplus was no longer valid, but many viewed revenue
sharing as a step toward a more rational system of fiscal federalism,
one in which revenue from a more progressive source of revenue
replaces or supplements revenue from a more regressive state–local
tax system. Some felt there was a need for revenue sharing as fiscal
relief for all state and local governments, while others felt it was an
absolutely necessary bailout of those in greatest need. By using per
capital income and tax effort in the formula, it was intended to be
somewhat redistributive and thus help the worst-off more, but not by
much. Still others accepted it in President Nixon's terms, as an antidote
to the centralized, regulated character of a federal aid system dominated by categorical grants. A few thought it could help pay for federal mandates.

Some critics pointed out that from a strict accounting point of view
there was no revenue to share, only a deficit. This argument relied
more on semantics than intellect. Those who argued that the separation
of taxation from spending was undesirable were overlooking the discretion that did exist within the huge grant-in-aid system already in place.
Lack of accountability seemed a hollow criticism of a program which
sought to promote creativity. As to the charge that state and local
governments had weaknesses, Congress and the Presidency would

soon endure scandals, including Watergate, which would remind everyone that not all corrupt government is state and local. The most valid criticism of revenue sharing from the congressional point of view may have been the one they were least likely to explicitly put forth, that they would lose the direct political credit which comes with categorical grants.

A presidential election in 1972 provided the primary political motivation, perhaps even turning the concept's biggest critic, Wilbur Mills, into a proponent. And an unprecedented lobby effort by state and local officials prodded a Congress that still needed the support of state and local officials for reelection. While there was devil in the details, as evidenced by the need to use two separate distribution formulas—one from the Senate and one from the House—the program eventually won broad, bipartisan support, even over the objection of members of Appropriations and other committees who felt threatened, either by the program itself or by its potential to start a trend. Indeed, it is interesting that the program strongly implied a criticism of the Congress for enacting the grant system it had. Much as with the Unfunded Mandates Relief Act and deficit reduction two decades later, the passage of revenue sharing importantly had Congress admitting that the whole of what they produced was maybe not as satisfying as the parts— that policy decisions that individually made for good politics may in sum have produced unacceptable outcomes.

Getting bipartisan support was not difficult. Democrats could support it because it would help cities, Democratic strongholds. For Republicans, it meshed nicely with the party's bias toward local government and was seen as an antidote to the social programs and centralizing strain of the Great Society. These incentives, along with presidential ambition, were enough to overcome the fiscal conservatism of both Richard Nixon and Congressman Mills, the two most important policy players. The program meant little to the public, already confused by the increasing "marbleization" of what had come to be termed Creative Federalism. Presenting General Revenue Sharing as "new money" reduced potential opposition from bureaucrats. Finally, and fortunately for proponents of General Revenue Sharing, there was also the perception that resources were available. The progressive federal income tax, fueled by inflation, had produced average annual increases of 13.1 percent between 1965 and 1970.[86]

With its manifest goals of providing general fiscal relief for state and local governments, and a shifting of decision-making power from Washington back to units of government closer to the people, General Revenue Sharing represented a major departure from the types of federal aid historically given. It was sold as a program whose results were expected to be noticeable, most optimistically producing, in the president's rhetoric, "a better way of solving problems," a "more creative" government, and a "new burst of creative energy throughout America." Yet the question of whether there might be latent goals of the program, including its use by a Republican president to help phase out the Great Society and dismantle the Democratic coalition of mayors and Washington officials, slightly dampened some of the enthusiasm of mayors and other local officials, who found themselves entering a period of changing and uncertain intergovernmental relations. It was under these conditions, then, that a highly hyped program was to meet a highly routinized local budgetary process.

NOTES

1. The analysis which follows relies greatly on *The Federalist Papers* (New York: Mentor Books, 1961) and The U.S. Advisory Commission on Intergovernmental Relations, *The Condition of Contemporary Federalism: Conflicting Theories and Collapsing Constraints* (Washington, DC: U.S. Government Printing Office, 1989).

2. *The Federalist Papers*, No. 39, p. 246.

3. United States Constitution, Amendment X.

4. Alfred H. Kelly and Winfred A. Harbison, *The American Constitution: Its Origins and Development*, 5th ed. (New York, NY: W.W. Norton and Company, 1976), p. 165.

5. U.S. Advisory Commission on Intergovernmental Relations, *The Condition of Contemporary Federalism*.

6. McCulloch v. Maryland, 4 Wheaton 316 (1819).

7. McCulloch v. Maryland, 4 Wheaton 316 (1819).

8. Gibbons v. Ogden, 9 Wheaton 1 (1824) and U.S. v. Darby Lumber, 312 U.S. 100 (1941), respectively.

9. Lloyd Free and Hadley Cantrill, *The Political Beliefs of Americans* (New York: Clarion Books, 1968), p. 80.

10. U.S. Advisory Commission on Intergovernmental Relations, "Financing Federal Growth: Changing Aspects of Fiscal Constraints," in *The Condition of Contemporary Federalism*, pp. 144–151.

11. Michael D. Reagan and John G. Sanzone, *The New Federalism*, 2nd ed. (New York: Oxford University Press, 1981), p. 54.

12. The discussion of grant history draws on several sources, most prominently Daniel Elazar, *The American Partnership: Intergovernmental Cooperation in the Nineteenth-Century United States* (Chicago: University of Chicago Press, 1962); W. Brooke Graves, *American Intergovernmental Relations: Their Origins, Historical Development, and Current Status* (New York: W.W. Norton and Co., 1970); Deil Wright, *Understanding Intergovernmental Relations*; and Richard D. Bingham, Brett W. Hawkins, and F. Ted Hebert, *The Politics of Raising State and Local Revenue* (New York: Praeger, 1978).

13. Bingham et al., *The Politics of*, p. 28.

14. Bingham et al., *The Politics of*, pp. 29–30.

15. 262 U.S. 447 (1923).

16. See National League of Cities v. Usery, 426 U.S. 833 (1976).

17. For an interesting alternative view on the Great Society and federal aid generally, see Frances Fox Piven and Richard A. Cloward, *Regulating the Poor: The Functions of Public Welfare* (New York: Vintage, 1971).

18. Aaron Wildavsky, *Speaking Truth to Power: The Art and Craft of Policy Analysis* (Boston: Little, Brown, and Co., 1979).

19. U.S. Advisory Commission on Intergovernmental Relations, *Significant Features of Fiscal Federalism—Vol. 2* (Washington, DC: Advisory Commission on Intergovernmental Relations, December 1994), p. 30.

20. Wright, *Understanding Intergovernmental Relations*, p. 136.

21. Bingham et al., *The Politics of*, p. 56.

22. Bingham et al., *The Politics of*, p. 58.

23. Wright, *Understanding Intergovernmental Relations*, p. 130.

24. Wright, *Understanding Intergovernmental Relations*, pp. 130–131.

25. *Inaugural Addresses of the Presidents of the United States from George Washington to Richard M. Nixon* (Washington, DC: U.S. Government Printing Office, 1974).

26. James A. Maxwell, U.S. Congress, Joint Economic Committee, *Revenue Sharing and its Alternatives: What Future for Fiscal Federalism?* (Washington, DC: U.S. Government Printing Office, 1967), p. 11.

27. "Editor's Notes," *Public Management* 55, no. 1 January 1923, inside cover.

28. Maxwell, *Revenue Sharing and its Alternatives*, p. 14.

29. Maureen McBreen, *Federal Revenue Sharing* (Washington, DC: The Library of Congress Legislative Reference Bureau, 1970).

30. Richard P. Nathan, *The Plot that Failed: Nixon and the Administrative Presidency* (New York: Wiley, 1975), p. 350. For other excellent summaries of the enactment of General Revenue Sharing, see Paul Dommel, *The Politics of Revenue Sharing* (Bloomington, IN: Indiana University Press, 1974; Will Myers, "A Legislative History of Revenue Sharing, *Annals, AAPSS*, May 1975, pp. 1–11; and Samuel H. Beer, "The Adoption of General Revenue Sharing: A Case Study in Public Sector Politics," *Public Policy* 24, no. 2, Spring 1970, pp. 127–195.

31. Interview with John Shannon, Washington, DC, October 10, 1996.

32. Interview with John Shannon.

33. Nixon Task Force Report of December 1968, cited in Richard P. Nathan *Monitoring Revenue Sharing*, (Washington, DC: Brookings Institute, 1975), p. 4.

34. "The President's Address to the Nation on Domestic Programs," *Weekly Compilation of Presidential Documents*, Vol. 5 (1969), pp. 1109–1110.

35. Interview with Jim Martin, Washington, DC, October 9, 1996.

36. Richard P. Nathan, *Monitoring Revenue Sharing*, p. 15.

37. "The State of the Union Message," January 22, 1971, p. 8.

38. "Revenue Sharing: Bitter Battle Looms in Congress, *Congressional Quarterly Weekly Report*, January 29, 1971, p. 213.

39. "Revenue Sharing," p. 213.

40. *Congressional Quarterly Weekly Report*, June 11, 1971, p. 1272.

41. U.S. Advisory Commission on Intergovernmental Relations, *Revenue Sharing—An Idea Whose Time Has Come* (Washington, DC: U.S. Government Printing Office, December 1970).

42. "Revenue Sharing," p. 213.

43. "Nixon's 'Six Great Goals': Some Hill Leaders Skeptical," *Congressional Quarterly Weekly Report*, January 29, 1971, p. 279.

44. "Revenue Sharing," *Congressional Quarterly Weekly Report*, June 11, 1971, p. 1272.

45. "New Funding Methods Considered for Federal Programs," *Congressional Quarterly Weekly Report*, January 24, 1969, p. 160.

46. Quoted in Robert Reischauer, "Revenue Sharing: Approaching the Crunch," draft, Brookings Institution, 1972, p. 8.

47. Paul Dommel, *The Politics of Revenue Sharing*.

48. Will S. Myers, "A Legislative History of Revenue Sharing," p. 3.

49. "Revenue Sharing: Bitter Battle . . . ," *Congressional Quarterly Weekly Report*, p. 217.

50. "Revenue Sharing," *Congressional Quarterly Weekly Report*, June 4, 1971, p. 1215.

51. "Revenue Sharing," *Congressional Quarterly Weekly Report*, June 4, 1971, p. 1215.

52. "Revenue Sharing," *Congressional Quarterly Weekly Report*, June 11, 1971, p. 1272.

53. "Revenue Sharing," *Congressional Quarterly Weekly Report*, June 11, 1971, p. 1274.

54. "Revenue Sharing," *Congressional Quarterly Weekly Report*, June 11, 1971, p. 1274.

55. The author's recollection.

56. "Revenue Sharing," *Congressional Quarterly Weekly Report*, August 12, 1972, p. 2017.

57. Robert Reischauer, "Revenue Sharing: Approaching the Crunch," draft paper, The Brookings Institution, 1972, p. 8.

58. "General Revenue Sharing: Giveaway or Godsend," *Congressional Quarterly Weekly*, May 6, 1972, p. 1000.

59. Dommel, *The Politics of Revenue Sharing*.

60. Donald Haider, *When Governments Come to Washington* (New York: MacMillan, 1974), p. 75.

61. "Text of Nixon's State of Union Address II," *Congressional Quarterly Weekly Report*, January 22, 1972, p. 121.

62. "General Revenue Sharing: Giveaway or Godsend?" *Congressional Quarterly Weekly Report*, May 6, 1972, p. 1003.

63. "Revenue Sharing: Bitter Battle . . ." *Congressional Quarterly Weekly Report*, January 29, 1971, p. 217.

64. United States Senate, Committee on Finance, *Report: Revenue Sharing Act of 1972*, Report 92–1050, Part I (Washington, DC: U.S. Government Printing Office, 1972).

65. Haider, *When Governments Come to Washington*, p. 74.

66. George D. Brown, "Beyond the New Federalism—Revenue Sharing in Perspective," *Harvard Journal of Legislation 15*, No. 1 (December 1977), p. 2.

67. Department of Treasury, *Regulations Governing the Payment of Initial Entitlements Under Title I of the State and Local Fiscal Assistance Act of 1972,"* (Washington, DC: U.S. Government Printing Office, 1972), p.6.

68. On this point see the testimony of Richard Nathan, *Hearings before the Subcommittee on Intergovernmental Relations of the Committee on Government Operations*, U.S. Senate, 93rd Congress, Second Session, Part I (Washington, DC: U.S. Government Printing Office, 1974), p. 424.

69. As quoted in Myers, "A Legislative History of Revenue Sharing," p. 8.

70. Meyers, "A Legislative History of Revenue Sharing," p. 8.

71. *Christian Science Monitor*, March 10, 1973, p.8.

72. "Revenue Sharing That Works," *The New Republic 164*, No. 22 (1971), p. 8.

73. "Revenue Sharing That Works," p. 7.

74. National League of Cities, "Background Paper and Chronology of Progress on Revenue Sharing," mimeograph, January 1969, cited in Haider, *When Governments Come to Washington*, p. 65.

75. Haider, *When Governments Come to Washington*, p. 271.

76. "Nixon's New Federalism Shapes the '74 Budget," *Business Week*, February 3, 1973, p. 58.

77. "Nixon's New Federalism . . .," p. 60.

78. Haider, *When Governments Come to Washington*, p. 272.

79. Only two of the six proposed consolidations passed, and in heavily modified form.

80. Haider, *When Governments Come to Washington*, p. 274. See also James G. Phillips, "New Federalism Report/Federal Budget Cuts Turn Mayors Against Administration Revenue Sharing," *National Journal Reports*, July 28, 1973, pp. 1103–1104.

81. Phillips, "New Federalism Report," p. 1102.

82. Phillips, "New Federalism Report," p. 1099.

83. Subcommittee on Intergovernmental Relations, *Hearings*, p. 524.

84. Subcommittee on Intergovernmental Relations, *Hearings*, p. 427; Dommel, *The Politics of Revenue Sharing*, p. 192.

85. "Nixon, Congress Still At Odds On Decentralizing Power," *Congressional Quarterly Weekly Report*, December 15, 1973, p. 3303.

86. U.S. Advisory Commission on Intergovernmental Relations, *Significant Features of Fiscal Federalism, vol. 2, 1994*, (Washington, DC: U.S. Advisory Commission on Intergovernmental Relations, 1994), Table 37, p. 72.

3

City Dynamics and Decisions: General Revenue Sharing at City Hall

Enactment of General Revenue Sharing was a dream come true for mayors and city managers, who eagerly awaited the arrival of the new unrestricted federal funds. The revenue was expected to allow officials in fiscally strained cities to avoid program cutbacks or perhaps allow new projects to be taken off the back burner, while those with healthier economies could stabilize taxes or undertake new initiatives. The rhetoric from Washington produced even higher hopes, suggesting that the new funds would reinvigorate the municipal budgeting process. Social science literature was less sanguine as to the possibility of a dramatic impact.

Making use of surveys of city chief executives over the life of the revenue sharing program allows an interesting story to unfold, one which for the most part might have been predicted, yet was not totally expected. This chapter will analyze their view of the impact of General Revenue Sharing in cities. It will most importantly examine how they said the funds were used and the process by which decisions were made, including the influence of the various participants. The issue of the use of revenue sharing in program areas which had traditionally been funded by federal categorical grants will be explored, as will other feelings of chief executives toward the program.

EXPECTATIONS—THE 1972 SURVEY

The passage of the General Revenue Sharing program was a much ballyhooed affair. Mayors and city managers had, through their professional associations as well as press accounts, been kept aware of and in many cases had been involved in the legislative struggle over this new form of federal aid. Thus before any funds actually appeared on the doorsteps of city halls, expectations as to the amount of funds to be received had been well-formed and they, in turn, had given birth to notions, both within and outside city government, as to their potential use.

In October 1972, before the first funds arrived, a questionnaire survey was sent to local chief executives in sixty-seven California cities and thirty-three New Jersey cities (Appendix). The California cities were all over 50,000 population, while the New Jersey cities were over 50,000 population and/or were members of the Legislative Action Committee of that state's Conference of Mayors—mostly Standard Metropolitan Statistical Area (SMSA) central cities as designated at the time by the U.S. Bureau of the Census. The response included fifty-eight California replies (87 percent) and twenty-five from New Jersey (75 percent), an 83 percent overall response rate.[1]

It was extremely important to gauge local opinion before the funds arrived, for two reasons. First, it would provide an unaffected view of what city chief executives expected the program to do, allowing comparison to the expectations of the policy makers in Washington, and thus determining whether communication between the two levels had led to realistic goals for the program. Second, conducting a survey before the funds had arrived would set a baseline of expectations of chief executives. Comparing these to outcomes of the initial budgeting of the funds would reveal the effects of local political participation and/or changing conditions.

The municipalities in the two states differed on predominant form of government. Of the fifty-eight California cities replying, fifty-four had a council–city manager form of government, while fourteen of the twenty-five New Jersey respondents functioned under the mayor–council system.

Anticipated Process

The reported process by which local decisions were to be made concerning the revenue sharing funds gave validity to the surveying of mayors and city managers. In sixty-nine of the eighty-two cities replying, the chief executives reported that they, themselves, would have the responsibility for drawing up the initial plans for the use of the funds (Table 3-1). City council members (six cities) and department heads (9 cities) were the other designees.[2] Overall, in seventy-four of the eighty-three cases, the process was to be a two-stepped one: chief executive program formulation with subsequent approval by another individual or body, usually the city council. This process is, of course, identical to the traditional municipal budgeting process.

The arrival of revenue sharing funds was expected to rejuvenate the local decision-making process, implying increased participation by

TABLE 3-1
Local Chief Executives Were To Be Responsible for Formulating
Initial Revenue-Sharing Plans

Primarily Responsible	Calif.	N.J.	Total
City Manager	48	5	53
Mayor	3	13	16
City Council	4	2	6
Department Head	5	4	9
	N = 58	N = 24	N = 82

citizen groups. Local chief executives were asked to note and rank anticipated sources of pressure in the allocation process for revenue-sharing funds. The results (Table 3-2) show that in California, with the city council/manager form of government dominant, local executives list the city council as by far the primary source of expected pressure, suggesting a relatively in-house allocation of revenue-sharing funds. In New Jersey cities, community groups were selected as the main source of anticipated local pressure, but by a narrow margin, with the

TABLE 3-2
Local Chief Executives Expect and Community Group and Council Pressure

	Source of Pressure—Ranked First		
	Calif.	N.J.	Total
City Council	27	7	34
Community Groups	7	9	16
Employee Unions	7	2	9
Department Heads	6	2	8
Other	0	0	0
	N = 47	N = 18	N = 55

	Source of Pressure—Mentioned		
	Calif.	N.J.	Total
Community Groups	45	20	65
City Council	48	15	63
Department Heads	35	15	50
Employee Unions	23	9	32
Other	4	3	7
	N = 58	N = 25	N = 83

city council again ranked highly. Combining the two states shows that the city council was clearly expected to be the prime source of pressure as to the use of the funds. Thus city chief executives did not expect the process for allocating revenue-sharing funds to significantly differ from that of the traditional budgetary process.

Anticipated Uses

The survey asked local chief executives to indicate the anticipated uses of their revenue sharing allocation for the first eighteen months of the program. They were given the following choices: "reduce property taxes," "expand existing services," "maintain existing services," "capital improvements," "initiate new programs," and "other." Respondents were asked to rank uses; while most did so, some only checked relevant uses. If only one category was checked, it was assigned a "first choice" status. The survey sought to record the expected general impact of the funds, rather than attempt to document their projected use in a strict accounting sense. Any attempt to have chief executives predict or later document actual dollar spending by area was thought to present a very difficult task, a viewpoint supported by other studies of the impact of General Revenue Sharing.

Among the choices offered, perhaps the most interesting phrasing involved "maintain existing services." Many analysts expected some of the General Revenue Sharing money to be substituted for locally raised revenue. (For example, instead of taxes being raised 10 percent the next year, they would be raised 5 percent and revenue sharing would fund the difference.) There was some concern in the design of the survey that some chief executives, given the controversy surrounding the program's passage, might not want to admit to using revenue sharing funds to substitute for local revenue. Hence the survey gave officials the politically safer choice "maintain existing services," implying that revenue sharing was providing funding to help a city to merely provide the services it already was providing, as well as the explicit "reduce property taxes" alternative.

Frequencies will be used throughout the chapter. In analyzing the survey results, as the reader will see, they tell the story as well as any other statistic. The lack of variation made determinants analysis challenging and, combined with the relatively small number of cities surveyed, produced poor measures of association.

The results of the first survey were very surprising (Table 3-3). The primary uses anticipated by officials within each state were remarkably consistent, yet there was great variation between cities in the two states. In California, 93 percent of those responding mentioned spending some revenue sharing funds on capital improvements, while of those ranking

TABLE 3-3
1972 Anticipated Uses: Intrastate Consensus, Interstate Diversity

California

Use	Mentioned	%	1st Choice	%
Capital Improvements	54	93%	39	76%
Expand Services	34	59%	2	3%
New Programs	32	55%	2	3%
Maintain Services	28	48%	6	12%
Reduce Taxes	19	33%	1	2%
	N = 58		N = 51	

New Jersey

Use	Mentioned	%	1st Choice	%
Reduce Taxes	21	84%	16	76%
Maintain Services	16	64%	1	5%
Expand Services	15	60%	1	5%
Capital Improvements	14	56%	3	14%
New Programs	12	48%	0	0
	N = 25		N = 21	

choices, 76 percent listed that use as their first priority.[3] In New Jersey, 84 percent of local chief executives expected to use some of the funding for property tax reduction, while 76 percent listed that use as their first choice for the funds.

It was remarkable that there was such a dominant first choice in each state; that is, that there was such consensus among local officials within each state as to the anticipated uses of the funds. Given the great social, economic, and political diversity of these cities, one might expect more variation. And it was equally surprising at first glance that the preferred use of the funds varied so greatly from one state to the other. We will return to these issues.

It is also important to note that the dominant first choices of the two states entailed very different priorities than those found in most of the federal categorical grant programs. These existing federal grant programs were generally more service-oriented; they would most likely have been represented in this survey by choices to expand and maintain existing services or even to initiate new programs.

Factors Affecting Expected Local Uses

What factors might explain the intrastate consensus and interstate contrast? The amazing "group-think" which initially occurred with each state, while at first surprising, is explainable.

Some analysts suggested that a city's expected predominant use of the first allocation for capital improvements could be a result of the fact that city budgets were already passed and in balance when the first funds arrived, producing a windfall which allowed lower priority construction or equipment projects to surface. While potentially explanatory in part, this argument is weakened by the fact that many cities had already anticipated receipt of funds in their most recent budget, and further were allowed twenty-four months to allocate the first payment. This issue was confronted directly in the second survey.

The more likely explanation for city officials in California expecting to use revenue sharing predominantly for capital improvements results from the stipulated five-year life of the program. This raises the spectrum of potential program termination, and from an administrative point of view this would tend to distort the allocation decisions of local officials. The initiation of new programs or the expansion of services under this scenario are to be avoided, as they would raise the expectations of the public or accustom them to services which would later have to be supported, if at all, out of general tax revenue. Most importantly, the creation of new jobs would be avoided, since the political repercussions of terminating employment are so great. Capital improvements offer the perfect hedge against an uncertain future. New buildings, facilities, and equipment purchased with revenue sharing funds would obviously still benefit the community, at relatively low local cost, if the program ended.

For these kinds of reasons, several of the professional journals of local government officials had recommended using the funds for capital improvements. *Public Management* noted:

> Due to the present short-term nature of the funding (five years), I have suggested to Claremont's (California) city council that it would be a mistake for the city to become dependent on revenue sharing for operating expenses such as salaries or hiring of additional employees, at least until the program develops a track record. I have suggested that the council consider limiting the expenditures from revenue sharing to low-maintenance capital outlays, experimental programs, and other non-recurring type expenditures, such as special studies.[4]

Similarly, the "Policy Guidelines" on use of revenue-sharing funds for the City of San Francisco stated, "Since General Revenue Sharing is a five-year program, low priority, except in special circumstances, should be given to projects which involve new personnel."[5] Finally, capital improvements also meet the political need for a highly visible, "concrete" impact. The potential for program termination thus seems to greatly prejudice the use of funds toward capital improvements for the local chief executive looking to reduce uncertainty.

Given these incentives for capital uses, how can we account for New Jersey's preference for property tax reduction? Fear of program termination would also suggest avoiding tax reductions, as that use, coupled with the end of the program, would likely result in the juxtaposition of large tax increases on a taxpaying public newly accustomed to lower taxes. In New Jersey, the lack of a state income tax and subsequent heavy reliance on the local property tax for city revenues was the determining variable, strong enough to overwhelm the disincentives. This point goes to the heart of state–local fiscal relations and gives validity to the claim made by some opponents of the revenue-sharing plan that it would keep a state like New Jersey from assuming full fiscal responsibility for its cities.

A Bureau of the Census report for 1968–1969 showed that the State of New Jersey was providing only half of what the average state was providing in aid to local governments (Table 3-4).[6] The State of California was giving nearly twice the percentage amount of financial support to its local governments than New Jersey, and nearly three times what New Jersey was giving in general local government support (unrestricted aid).

This lack of support had an important impact on the finances of New Jersey cities. Property taxes accounted for 31.7 percent of all city general revenues nationwide in 1972, and stood at 25.9 percent for cities in the State of California.[7] New Jersey cities, with less state aid and fewer revenue options, were forced to rely on the property tax for 54.8 percent of their general revenues. This reliance on the property tax is particularly extreme. Effective property tax rates in some New Jersey cities hovered in the 8 percent range during this period. Paying the entire value of your home in property taxes every twelve years or so is burdensome, especially in the case of a tax which at the time usually required a lump-sum payment.

The U.S. Advisory Commission on Intergovernmental Relations occasionally calculates tax effort for various tax instruments by state,

TABLE 3-4
Total State Aid to Local Governments

	As a % of General Revenue from Local Own Sources	General Local Government Support
California	53.4%	5.13%
New Jersey	29.1%	1.77%
National Average	54.0%	8.63%

a measure of actual taxes collected as a percentage of a nationally compared tax capacity, or tax base. In 1971, the year preceding the arrival of revenue sharing funds, the property tax effort of New Jersey local governments was calculated at 175, dwarfing the national average of 100, and California's 106.[8] Mayors and city administrators had to be sensitive to this. In fact, as tax effort is one of the elements of the distribution formula to cities, New Jersey officials were willing, by reducing taxes, to receive a lessened General Revenue Sharing allocation in following years. And, of course, they were clearly willing to place themselves in the unenviable position of having to impose large tax increases in the future, should the revenue sharing program be terminated. The choice should not have been an easy one.

It would appear, then, that New Jersey's heavy reliance on property taxes resulted in a near-statewide consensus on the need for tax reduction and the anticipated use of revenue sharing funds to accomplish it. A high level of property taxation resulted in uniform decisions to pursue property tax reduction no matter what the disincentives. The consensus to reduce taxes may be seen as resulting from the fact that property taxes had become an, if not the, important political issue in New Jersey, and it shows that state–local tax structure is an extremely important variable in local expenditure decisions.

Specific Expenditure Areas

City chief executives were asked to anticipate the specific expenditure areas in which revenue sharing funds would be spent. Of particular interest was a comparison of expected General Revenue Sharing uses with the outcomes of the traditional budgeting process, and further contrasting them with the types of expenditures representative of federal categorical grants, which were about to come under increased scrutiny by a suddenly deficit-sensitive Nixon Administration.

The ranking of proposed expenditure areas differed a little between the two states (Table 3-5). Although there was general agreement on a need for expenditures for public safety, the fact that California's number one overall priority involved parks and recreation seemed indicative of a more relaxed financial condition. In comparison to other types of programs needed by urban residents, this choice might be considered a relative luxury by some. For those who viewed revenue sharing as a necessary response to an urban fiscal crisis, this use was more than a little surprising.

In New Jersey, the most often mentioned expenditure area was public safety, and by a fairly wide margin. This is one of the leading expenditure areas of all cities, and for New Jersey also likely reflects

TABLE 3-5
California and New Jersey Cities Differ in Anticipated Expenditure Areas

California	Mentioned	%	1st Choice	%
Parks & Recreation	39	67%	12	29%
Public Works	34	59%	11	26%
Public Safety	33	57%	11	26%
Environmental Protection	26	45%	2	5%
Libraries	19	33%	1	2%
General Govt., Dept.	15	16%	3	7%
Public Transit	7	12%	1	2%
Housing	6	10%	0	0%
Health	5	9%	0	0%
General Govt., Non-Dept.	4	7%	1	2%
	N = 58		N = 42	

New Jersey	Mentioned	%	1st Choice	%
Public Safety	18	72%	10	59%
Public Works	11	44%	1	6%
Health	10	40%	0	0%
Parks & Recreation	9	36%	0	0%
General Govt., Dept.	7	28%	2	12%
General Govt., Non-Dept.	5	20%	3	18%
Libraries	4	16%	0	0%
Housing	2	8%	0	0%
Environmental Protection	2	8%	1	6%
Public Transit	1	4%	0	0%
	N = 25		N = 17	

the power of employee unions and the less comfortable position of its cities. Urban flight had occurred in the East long before it became prominent in the West.

How do these expected priorities compare to the allocations of city budgets the previous year? In California cities, five of the top six rankings overlap, with the primary difference being the jump in the ranking of parks and recreation from fifth in budget allocation to first in use of revenue sharing funds.[9] For New Jersey cities, and allowing for consideration of the health category under the city budget reporting category "health and local welfare," all six of the top expected uses of revenue sharing funds matched the previous year's expenditure pattern.[10] The specific uses in both states suggested, then, that expected functional allocations of revenue sharing funds would to a great extent mirror normal budget allocations, initially confirming the hypothesis that use of the new federal funds would not produce dramatic changes in local budget outcomes nor substitute for announced reductions in federal categorical aid. Housing and mass transit, for example, two areas in which the federal government has been extremely active, were given particularly low expected use scores.

Conclusions on Expected Impact

While President Nixon and congressional policy makers claimed that the General Revenue Sharing program would generate a great deal of enthusiasm and rejuvenate the decision-making process of local governments, the initial survey found the allocation process expected in California and New Jersey cities to mirror the annual budget process. Further, while local chief executives in some cities expected community pressure as to the use of the funds, the city council was the most often mentioned source, as might have been expected. It would appear that the actors traditionally dominant in local budgeting—city council members, department heads, and the chief executive—would have the greatest influence.

Nor were the expected outcomes particularly exciting. California's predominant use for capital improvements appeared mostly a product of fear generated by the initial five-year life of the program, while New Jersey's emphasis on property tax reduction was clearly a result of that state's tax structure. Neither of these uses were leading rationales for the program's passage; General Revenue Sharing might not have passed had they been. Would there be a "burst of creative energy" which would enable local officials to better identify and meet local needs? It was hard to expect a burst of creative energy, given the data from this survey.

Overall, what Washington expected and what local chief executives in these two states expected were very different things. This contradiction suggests either a lack of communication between officials at the two levels, perhaps selective testimony by local officials as to expected use of the funds, and/or selective hearing by members of Congress eager to gain support for passage.

The tremendous importance and impact of the state–local tax structure in New Jersey also shows the potential for a federal aid program to have wildly differing effects in different states. This makes intergovernmental policy making more difficult.

As to the broader research questions posed in the first chapter, it appeared from the initial survey that the traditional municipal budget process and its actors would overwhelm this new federal aid program.

The uses expected along with the specific functional expenditure area allocations bore this out. The size of this new budgetary increment, in inflationary times, would also likely lessen its impact. New Jersey and California cities had experienced local budget increases of 17 percent and 11 percent in the fiscal year preceding passage of the program; General Revenue Sharing funds comprised only approximately 5 percent of each city's budget, and therefore was unlikely to produce a big impact.

Were local chief executives in these two states expecting to use revenue sharing funds to substitute for announced cutbacks in federal categorical aid? Neither of the two primary anticipated uses, property tax reduction and capital improvements, nor the dominant functional expenditure areas of parks and recreation, public safety, and public works, would offer any evidence of this occurring. Nor should this be surprising. The whole purpose of matching, categorical grant-in-aid programs is to stimulate state and local spending in areas which are determined by Congress to be in the national interest, and which state and local officials may not have been providing on their own.

Different results might have occurred had General Revenue Sharing been implemented before the glut of Great Society programs. As it was, however, a psychological reliance on federal grants in certain areas had formed. The City of San Francisco listed as one of its guidelines for determining use of revenue sharing funds the following: "Because the City should insist on continued Federal and State Support, General Revenue Sharing should not be used extensively for programs currently financed by categorical grants."[11] Clearly, local chief executives were working in an uncertain intergovernmental aid environment, and their expected use of the funds was meant to "send a message" to Washington. Local budgeting would become intergovernmental politics.

Data collected in the second survey, conducted after the funds had arrived, shed further light on many of these issues.

INITIAL IMPACTS—THE 1974 SURVEY

On December 11, 1972, the first revenue sharing allocations were sent to local governments across the United States. Those checks covered the first half of calendar year 1972, and within four months cities had received payments equaling a full fifteen months of their entitlement. While first planned use reports were due at the Treasury Department's Office of Revenue Sharing on June 30, cities by law had twenty-four months from receipt of the funds to use the new revenue.

In April 1974, a second survey was sent to the chief executives of the sixty-seven California and thirty-three New Jersey cities previously contacted. It had been over a year since revenue sharing funds had arrived, and cities had gone through one normal budget cycle since the first survey was conducted. The initial impact of the new federal program was by now clear.

The overall response to the second survey was even better than the first. While New Jersey's response rate dipped slightly to 70 percent, California cities responded at a 94 percent rate, producing an overall response of 86 percent.

Process

The process reportedly used to allocate revenue sharing funds was, as had been expected, similar in the two states, with members of the executive branch most often drawing up the initial plans and with ultimate approval by the city council. Again, this procedure mirrors that documented by studies of the traditional municipal budget process.[12]

Survey responses indicated that by a margin of 82–3 cities in the survey did not "establish a separate office or staff to administer revenue sharing funds." Further, 76 percent of respondents (63 of 83) admitted that the decision-making process used to allocate revenue-sharing funds was not kept separate from the regular budget process. Clearly, the great majority of cities treated even the initial allocation as normal revenue. Twenty-seven cities (31 percent) said that they did not hold hearings on the allocation of revenue sharing funds at all. As Earl Harris, president of the Newark City Council, said in an interview, "We proceeded in the same way as usual."

In terms of pressure as to the use of the funds, community groups and city council remained the top two sources overall (Table 3-6). In comparing the responses with the anticipated pressure noted in Survey I (Table 3-2), some interesting trends were evident, however. In California, there was a substantial decline in the number of chief executives rating pressure by the city council as the primary source of pressure, accompanied by a significant increase in the number of chief executives experiencing community group pressure. Clearly, community groups in California were more energized by the arrival of revenue sharing funds than local chief executives had anticipated.

On the other coast, there was a substantial reduction in the number of New Jersey cities recording citizen pressure at all. New Jersey's variation from expectations may be a result of the previously noted consensus in that state as to the use of funds for tax reduction; by announcing the use of funds for property tax reduction, officials there may have preempted the need for community groups to get involved.

An explanation for the contrasting trend in the two states regarding council pressure may also lie in the respective forms of government.

TABLE 3-6
Chief Executives Experienced Community Group and City Council Pressure

	Source of Pressure—Ranked First		
	CA	NJ	Total
City Council	18	12	30
Community Groups	21	2	23
Department Heads	17	1	18
Unions	2	1	3
Other	2	1	3
	N = 60	N = 17	N = 77

	Source of Pressure—Mentioned		
	CA	NJ	Total
Community Groups	41	5	46
City Council	33	15	48
Department Heads	32	6	38
Unions	9	1	10
Other	2	2	4
	N = 63	N = 23	N = 86

In New Jersey's mayor–council system, antagonism is built into the process; the decline in city council pressure in California may conversely be a function of the close working relationship the city manager must have with city council members.

Actual Uses

The second survey asked local chief executives, "To what purpose(s) was the amount allocated to your city *for the first 18 months put?*" The choices, again, were "reduce property taxes," "expand existing services," "maintain existing services," "capital improvements," "initiate new programs," and "other." Respondents were asked to rank uses; once more, while most did so, some only checked relevant uses.

The results of the second survey, like the first, displayed intrastate consensus as to initial uses and interstate diversity (Table 3-7). In California, 90 percent of city managers report using some of the funds for capital improvements, with 76 percent designating such a use as the primary use. New Jersey's chief executives reported two dominant uses, property tax reduction and the maintenance of existing services,

TABLE 3-7
First Allocation Uses: California and New Jersey Differ

California

Use	Mentioned	%	1st Choice	%
Capital Improvements	57	90%	45	76%
Maintain Services	30	48%	11	19%
Initiate New Programs	29	46%	0	0%
Expand Services	19	30%	2	3%
Reduce Property Taxes	3	5%	0	0%
	N = 63		N = 58	

New Jersey

Use	Mentioned	%	1st Choice	%
Maintain Services	16	70%	9	43%
Reduce Property Taxes	15	65%	9	43%
Expand Services	9	39%	1	5%
Capital Improvements	6	26%	2	10%
Initiate New Programs	6	26%	0	0%
	N = 23		N = 21	

representing together 86 percent of the first choice uses listed. Since use to maintain existing services can be viewed as a pseudonym for local revenue substitution, by far the predominant use of revenue sharing funds in New Jersey was the relief of local property tax pressure.

Comparison of the results on actual use to the expectations recorded in the first survey (Table 3-3) suggests that local chief executives were able to predict and were most likely in control of the allocation decisions. They were not greatly swayed by any outside pressure, at least in the broad sense, even with the increase in community group pressure. In New Jersey, while the "maintain existing services" use rises greatly and the number listing property tax reduction as the first choice falls, 81 percent of the chief executives had predicted tax substitution purposes (property tax reduction and maintain services) as their first choice for use of revenue sharing funds, compared to the 86 percent whose cities actually did so. In California, capital improvements were listed as the first choice of 76 percent of chief executives in both the "expectations" and "actual use" surveys.

Again, none of these predominant uses suggest a reinvigorated decision-making process. Further evidence of the lack of innovation is found in the drop in both states from expected to actual use of the "expand existing services" and "initiate new programs" categories, neither ranked highly in the first place. If community group pressure was successful, it would appear that local chief executives correctly anticipated their wishes. This is more likely to have been true in New Jersey, where perhaps most were in favor of tax reduction, but it is less likely in California, where desire for capital improvements is not as likely to be so uniform among community groups. Also worth noting in California is a slight first choice increase for "maintain existing services" from Survey I to Survey II, suggesting that some revenue substitution was occurring there.

Respondents were also asked, "To what purpose(s) was the amount allocated to your city for the [then] most recent fiscal year (FY 1974) put?" In California, while capital improvements remains the most frequently mentioned use and the leading first choice, the tabulation shows a dramatic increase in the "maintain existing services" category, especially as a first choice (Table 3-8). Thus the gap between uses in the two states narrows some in the second year's allocation. Further declines in the "expand existing services" and "initiate new programs" uses were also recorded by California chief executives, although two

TABLE 3-8
Second Allocation Uses: The Differences Narrow

California

Use	Mentioned	%	1st Choice	%
Capital Improvements	50	79%	29	50%
Maintain Services	37	59%	23	40%
Initiate New Programs	21	33%	2	3%
Expand Services	13	21%	2	3%
Reduce Property Taxes	3	5%	0	0%
Other	2	3%	2	3%
	N = 63		N = 58	

New Jersey

Use	Mentioned	%	1st Choice	%
Maintain Services	15	65%	7	32%
Reduce Property Taxes	14	61%	9	41%
Capital Improvements	7	30%	4	18%
Expand Services	7	30%	2	9%
Initiate New Programs	1	4%	0	0%
	N = 23		N = 22	

cities did report a first-choice use of revenue sharing funds for new programs.

In New Jersey's second fiscal year allocations, "maintain services" and "reduce property taxes" remained the most frequently mentioned categories, still comprising 73 percent of the first-choice uses. There was also a slight increase in capital improvement uses, as well as the continued decline in the "new programs" and "expand services" selections. In fact, the use of revenue sharing funds in New Jersey for new programs dropped dramatically from the expectations survey to the second use period—from a mention in 48 percent of the cities to a mere 4 percent incidence. Coupled with the decline for this use in California, the evidence suggests that whatever innovativeness may accompany a program of revenue sharing at its debut, however small, is likely to decline even further as time wears on.

Factors Affecting Local Uses

In the second survey, New Jersey executives encountered such a low level of community pressure that generalizations about its effect on use are relatively meaningless. But given the increase in community pressure in California, with 65 percent experiencing some pressure and 35 percent listing them as the prime claimant on the use of the funds, it is interesting to try to gauge its impact.

Comparisons were made between uses in those California cities which experienced pressure group activity and the total sample (Table 3-9). For the first allocation, while the ranking of actual uses of revenue sharing funds remains the same, city chief executives in those cities experiencing community group pressure reported sizeable increases in use of revenue sharing funds for new programs. This suggests that some groups did mobilize around the receipt of revenue sharing funds, while others seeking to protect existing programs may have produced some of the increased tendency to maintain existing services. In the second full year allocation, the trend continues, with "maintain" and "new programs" incidence up significantly in cities with community pressure (Table 3-10). These findings suggested that it would be worthwhile to correlate uses overall with uses in those California cities whose chief executives ranked community group pressure first in terms of activity. For the first allocation period, the two largest increases for cities with community groups recognized as the prime source of pressure were again in the "maintain" and "new program" uses (Table 3-11). By the next allocation, however, there was a substantially higher incidence of the "maintain" use (Table 3-12). These data suggest that, while some community groups may have been successful early in

TABLE 3-9
First Allocation: Effect of Community Group Pressure Not Great in California

Use Without Community Pressure	Mentioned	%
Capital Improvements	19	83%
Maintain Services	7	30%
Initiate New Programs	6	26%
Expand Services	6	26%
Reduce Property Taxes	0	0
	N = 23	

Use With Community Pressure	Mentioned	%
Capital Improvements	38	95%
Maintain Services	23	58%
Initiate New Programs	23	58%
Expand Services	13	33%
Reduce Property Taxes	3	7%
	N = 40	

TABLE 3-10
Second Allocation: Effect of Community Group Pressure in California

Use Without Community Pressure	Mentioned	%
Capital Improvements	17	77%
Maintain Services	8	37%
Initiate New Programs	3	14%
Expand Services	5	23%
Reduce Property Taxes	2	9%
Other	1	5%
	N = 22	

Use With Community Pressure	Mentioned	%
Capital Improvements	33	80%
Maintain Services	29	71%
Initiate New Programs	18	44%
Expand Services	8	20%
Reduce Property Taxes	1	2%
Other	1	2%
	N = 41	

TABLE 3-11
First Allocation: Effect of Community Group Pressure
Ranked First

Use Without Community Pressure	Ranked First	%
Capital Improvements	38	90%
Maintain Services	18	43%
Initiate New Programs	18	44%
Expand Services	12	29%
Reduce Property Taxes	2	5%
	N = 42	

Use With Community Pressure	Ranked First	%
Capital Improvements	19	90%
Maintain Services	12	57%
Initiate New Programs	11	52%
Expand Services	7	33%
Reduce Property Taxes	1	5%
	N = 21	

TABLE 3-12
Second Allocation: Community Group Pressure Ranked First
Increases the Maintain Services Use in California

Use Without Community Pressure	Ranked First	%
Capital Improvements	33	79%
Maintain Services	21	50%
Initiate New Programs	13	31%
Expand Services	9	22%
Reduce Property Taxes	3	7%
Other	2	5%
	N = 42	

Use With Community Pressure	Ranked First	%
Maintain Services	17	81%
Capital Improvements	16	76%
Initiate New Programs	8	38%
Expand Services	4	19%
Reduce Property Taxes	0	0%
Other	3	14%
	N = 21	

getting new programs adopted, over the even slightly longer run either there was less revenue room for new programs or the already established groups were better able to defend their program base.[13]

Explanation

It was argued in analysis of the first survey on expectations that California city preference for capital improvements was related to uncertainty over the revenue sharing program's future. Fear of having to continue any new program or services with locally raised revenue would lead officials to put as much of the funds as possible into nonrecurring expenses, and capital improvements provided such a vehicle. Reducing the potentially negative fallout of funding cutbacks was the guiding principle.

This rationale was documented by other observers at the time. Richard Nathan, who headed the Brookings Institution study of the impact of revenue sharing, testified before Congress that "realizing that the program was funded for less than five years, many communities decided to place their entitlements into non-recurring capital expenditures that would not financially obligate their budgets beyond 1976."[14] Mayor Moon Landrieu of New Orleans concurred ". . . they spent all of their money in one-time projects, some because that is where the need was the greatest, others because they feared that the program would not be continued, not only after the five years, but would not be continued beyond 1 year."[15]

Data collected in the second survey bear out this analysis. Local chief executives were asked, "If revenue sharing were to be discontinued, in what way would you allocate your last allocation?" Comparing the responses (Table 3-13) to the second allocation uses (Table 3-8) proves interesting. In New Jersey, the only increase is a 13 percent increase in the number of chief executives mentioning capital improvements as their last use. For California cities, the ranking of last uses is very similar to the most recent allocation, suggesting that they were already spending it as if the program were to be terminated soon. "Initiate new programs" does drop dramatically in California, reaffirming the view that new programs are to be avoided when facing revenue uncertainty. Interesting trends also include a slight increase in the maintain category in California and significant percentage drops in the expand services category in both states.

Clearly, California executives do not want to be saddled with ongoing expenses due to, but no longer funded by, revenue sharing. This is also evident in responses given by officials in both states to the query, "What, in your opinion, is the politically 'safest' use of revenue sharing funds?" Choices offered were "reduce taxes," "capital improvements,"

TABLE 3-13
Last Allocation Would Favor Capital and Maintain Uses

California

Uses	Mentioned	%
Capital Improvements	47	75%
Maintain Services	41	65%
Expand Services	9	14%
Reduce Property Taxes	3	11%
Initiate New Programs	3	11%
	N = 63	

New Jersey

Uses	Mentioned	%
Maintain Services	14	61%
Capital Improvements	10	43%
Reduce Property Taxes	10	43%
Expand Services	4	17%
Initiate New Programs	2	9%
	N = 23	

"new programs," "new jobs," "maintain services," "increase existing services," and "other." The leading first choice of the sixty-three California chief executives answering this question was capital improvements, indicated by forty-seven, followed by twenty-one for maintain services and thirteen for reduce taxes. Of the sixty-three, none listed new jobs or new programs.

But maybe California local chief executives don't believe in new programs and expanded services anyway. A question was asked which sought to record the uses which the chief executives themselves thought would ultimately be most beneficial to their city. Comparing these "ideal" uses to the second allocation (Table 3-8) shows that these executives mention expanding existing services 44 percent more often than actually undertaken, reducing property taxes 33 percent more often, and initiating new programs 21 percent more frequently (Table 3-14). It is plain that fear of program termination was a distorting factor in use decisions in California cities.

One final hypothesis regarding California city preference for capital improvements involved the fact that initial revenue sharing funds arrived in the middle of the local fiscal year. It could be argued that the funds could therefore be used to fund back-burner projects; cities often have a wish list of capital expenditures. In addition to the continued

TABLE 3-14
"Ideal" Uses

New Jersey

Use	Mentioned	%	First Choice	%
Capital Improvements	17	74%	7	33%
Reduce Property Taxes	15	65%	10	48%
Expand Services	12	52%	1	5%
Initiate New Programs	10	43%	0	0%
Maintain Services	7	39%	3	14%
	N = 23		N = 21	

California

Use	Mentioned	%	First Choice	%
Capital Improvements	56	89%	31	53%
Expand Services	41	65%	8	14%
Maintain Services	36	57%	13	22%
Initate New Programs	34	54%	5	9%
Reduce Property Taxes	24	38%	0	0%
	N = 63		N = 58	

high incidence of the capital improvements use in the second allocation period, during the regular budget cycle, other data gathered in the second survey helped to refute this position. Local chief executives were directly asked whether, given the program's imminent passage, they had anticipated revenue sharing funds in their FY 1973 budget. In California, 74 percent of local chief executives indicated that they had done so.

How, then, can we account for the increase in California in the use of revenue sharing funds to maintain existing services over the course of the 1972–1974 period? Two hypotheses seem equally plausible. First, as has been noted throughout, the "maintain" use has been associated with property tax pressure and worsened financial condition. California, while not even close to the property tax pressure level of New Jersey, was beginning in the early 1970s to experience upward pressure on property values and hence assessments, producing real tax increases as local officials were slow to lower rates. All of this later resulted, as we know, in the property tax revolt of Proposition 13.[16]

For the harder pressed cities, the situation was already bad, leading Meltsner and Wildavsky, for example, to write about 1969 Oakland "The local property tax, the main source of revenue for cities, is exhausted in a political if not economic sense. The common perception among officials is that 'we cannot raise the property tax rate.' "[17] Other California cities may have begun to catch Oakland by 1974.

Nathan's study of revenue sharing concurred:

> Our data indicates that there has been a substantial substitution effect in the use of shared revenue. That is to say, significant amounts of these funds have been used—not for new spending—but to cut taxes, hold down taxes, balance the budget, or avoid borrowing which otherwise would have been undertaken.[18]

Chief executives in California, then, were most likely using an increasing share of their funds to substitute for local property tax increases.

An alternative hypothesis for the increasing use of revenue sharing to maintain services in California, while not contradictory, relates more to the program itself. As was noted, innovative uses declined from expectations to the 1974 allocation. Interviews with local officials revealed that by the second year of the program, the funds it delivered were indeed often being treated as general revenue, and therefore allocated, as most city budgets are, to meet the rising costs of doing what the city had been doing the year before. In fact, two mutually reenforcing trends drove the use of revenue sharing funds toward the "maintain" use: the increasing costs of operating at last year's level of service, due to inflation, and the decreasing purchasing power of the revenue sharing allocations over time, as those payments remained fixed.

These same two hypotheses easily explain the increased use of revenue sharing funds to maintain services in New Jersey. The property tax pressure argument is, of course, even more relevant here. While property tax reduction may have been politically necessary at first, given the publicity surrounding revenue sharing's arrival, even that use became a luxury as fiscal pressure mounted. Mayor Kenneth Gibson of Newark testified before Congress that:

> In fact, the cost of maintaining basic services has become so high that it is slowly strangling urban America. Most cities have only one means of raising the money they need to maintain basic services. I say in most cities, and I am talking about our area, particularly New Jersey. This is the property tax. With no other alternative, city after city has faced the unpleasant prospect of cutting vital services or raising the property tax.[19]

He continued:

> And the problem perpetuates itself. The higher we are forced to raise taxes to provide basic services, the more businesses and homeowners are forced

to leave the city. This means fewer jobs, greater demands on city services, and fewer ratables to provide these services.

If we were to cut down on the delivery of services, the result would be the same. More business and homeowners would be forced to leave, and either way, fewer new businesses and developers would be interested in coming in to assist us to rebuild our cities.

Mr. Chairman, general revenue sharing is the only form of Federal assistance that enables urban areas to break this cycle; that is, to maintain basic services without destroying the ratable base upon which the future social and economic prosperity of our cities depends.[20]

As in California, a look at the ideal uses (Table 3-14) noted by New Jersey executives reveals that compared to the actual allocation in 1974, there is a 35 percent more frequent incidence of the maintain services use than they would have liked.

Further analysis of this uninhibited discretion table (3-14) lends further evidence that New Jersey cities were not using revenue sharing as they would have hoped to. While maintain drops and reduce taxes remains mentioned about as frequently in moving from actual to ideal uses, capital improvements are mentioned 44 percent more frequently as an ideal use, new programs 34 percent more often, and would expand existing services registers a 22 percent rise. Clearly New Jersey officials have preferred, in a world with more financial support from the state and less reliance on the property tax, to use revenue sharing funds for other purposes.

Two other bits of data offer support and explain the decision of New Jersey chief executives to augment local revenue, and also produce additional evidence of the impact of the contrast in reliance on the property tax in New Jersey versus California. Survey respondents were asked to note the chief problem facing their city. In New Jersey, 43 percent of local chief executives designated inadequate revenue as their first choice, compared to 28 percent of the cities responding in California. In response to the politically safest use of the funds, 52 percent of New Jersey officials listed property tax reduction as the first choice, compared to only 11 percent in California. When interviewed on the use of revenue sharing funds in his city, Newark City Council President Harris said: "People got a reduction in taxes. That's their biggest complaint."

Specific Expenditure Areas

Local chief executives in the two states were asked to indicate the specific expenditure areas to which their first two years of revenue-sharing funds had been devoted. As was true of the expectations survey, the three most frequently mentioned areas in the two states were similar—public safety, parks and recreation, and public works (Table 3-15). In New Jersey, public safety uses represented 90 percent of first choice uses, while in California, public safety and parks and recreation comprised 78 percent of the top priorities. The top three expenditure areas in each state involve services which traditionally have been the largest and most important service-oriented expenditures at the municipal government level. Again, comparison of the ranked uses with the results of recent budget outcomes for cities in each state finds that these three expenditure areas were among the five largest budget accounts.[21] It is also worth noting again that the two functional areas with perhaps the most federal support available, housing and public transit, had been studiously avoided by local revenue sharing decision makers.

Did the predictions made by local chief executives in the first survey hold up? Comparing the actual first allocations with those listed as expectations once again provided evidence that these officials were fairly firmly in control of revenue sharing allocation decisions. The top three areas remained the same within each state, although parks and recreation took over second place in mention in New Jersey while public safety did the same in California. The latter change may well be tied to that state's increased use of revenue sharing funds to maintain existing services. In the second allocation period, little change occurs in mentions among the top three, although public safety arrives in first place in California as a first choice use. Public works drops a little percentage-wise in both states, probably paralleling the decline in use for capital improvement purposes.

Finally, the federally aided areas of housing and transportation remained at or near the bottom of the priority list. This corresponds to local chief executive response to the question in the second survey, "Which level of government should have primary responsibility for provision of each of the following services?" (Table 3-16). Clearly, a division of responsibility between these two levels of government had been established in the minds of local chief executives.

While cutbacks in categorical aid in no way approached President Nixon's announced intentions, there were some federal funding losses and a good deal of impoundment experienced by cities. Interviews conducted with local chief executives in the two states overwhelmingly revealed a belief on their part that federal categorical funding had indeed been cut, no matter what the facts. The second survey gave these officials an opportunity to comment directly on the substitution for cuts in federal categorical aid issue.

TABLE 3-15
Public Safety, Public Works, and Parks and Recreation are Chief
Expenditure Areas

New Jersey

Expenditure Area	First Allocation			
	Mentioned	%	1st Choice	%
Public Safety	20	90%	17	85%
Parks and Recreation	12	60%	1	5%
Public Works	9	45%		
Environmental Protection	7	35%	2	10%
General Government Dept.	7	35%		
Health	6	30%		
Library	5	25%		
Public Transit	1	5%		
General Gov't, Non-Dept.	0			
Housing	0			

Expenditure Area	Second Allocation			
	Mentioned	%	1st Choice	%
Public Safety	20	90%	17	85%
Parks and Recreation	9	45%	1	5%
Public Works	7	35%		
General Government Dept.	7	35%		
Health	7	35%		
Environmental Protection	6	30%	1	5%
Library	4	25%	1	5%
Public Transit	1	5%		
General Gov't. Non-Dept.	0			
Housing	0			
	N = 22		N = 20	

Continued

Officials were asked, "Has uncertainty over the federal government's intentions in the area of categorical grant programs influenced your use of revenue sharing funds?" An affirmative answer came from 28 percent of chief executives responding. Thirty-nine of eighty-one respondents (58 percent) claimed that their city had experienced "cutbacks in funding in federal categorical programs in the last eighteen months."

The next query posed was, "Have you used any general revenue sharing funds to replace money cut back in federal categorical pro-

TABLE 3-15
Continued

California

Expenditure Area	First Allocation			
	Mentioned	*%*	*1st Choice*	*%*
Parks and Recreation	47	78%	21	40%
Public Safety	44	73%	20	38%
Public Works	31	52%	7	13%
General Gov't, Non-Dept.	18	30%	1	2%
Environmental Protection	12	20%		
Library	12	20%		
Public Transit	11	18%	2	4%
Health	8	13%		
General Government Dept.	5	8%	2	4%
Housing	1	2%		
	N = 60		*N = 53*	

Expenditure Area	Second Allocation			
	Mentioned	*%*	*1st Choice*	*%*
Parks and Recreation	42	70%	13	27%
Public Safety	41	68%	20	41%
Public Works	22	37%	8	16%
Library	18	30%	2	4%
General Government Dept.	17	28%	2	4%
Environmental Protection	9	15%		
Public Transit	8	13%	1	2%
General Gov't, Non-Dept.	6	10%	3	6%
Health	6	10%		
Housing	4	2%		
	N = 60		*N = 49*	

grams?" Nineteen said that they had done so. The respondents who had replied that they had not were given one final query: "If 'No,' has it been due to program failures or a desire to force continued federal support?" While only sixteen chief executives responded to this question, three-fourths (twelve) said the reason for failure to devote revenue sharing money to fill in for cutbacks in categorical aid was "a desire to force continued federal support."

So it appears that a new type of lobbying was at work. Some local chief executives, desirous of continued federal support in the

TABLE 3-16
Local Chief Executives Assign Program Responsibility

Local		Federal	
Public Safety	78	Housing	35
Parks and Recreation	77	Environmental Protection	34
Libraries	76	Public Transit	22
Public Works	75	Manpower	20
Roads	66	Roads	15
Education	48	Public Works	12
Health	45	Health	12
Manpower	45	Parks and Recreation	10
Housing	41	Education	5
Public Transit	41	Public Safety	3
Environmental Protection	36	Libraries	2
	N = 88		N = 88

categorical areas and wanting to hold President Nixon to his promise that revenue sharing was "new" money, purposely avoided giving the federal government signals that they would pick up responsibility for scaled-back programs. There are at least three rationales for this insistence. The first is tradition or habit. Local governments had come to expect the federal government to provide certain programs at certain levels of funding. The second results from the general rule of city officials to maximize federal aid dollars, as noted by Wright and Pressman, among others.[22] Finally, Pressman also makes the argument that local chief executives like being able to blame the federal government at times for programs which benefit a minority of city residents, which may be objectionable to the majority and/or which may be opposed by local political elites.[23] In any case, it is clear that decisions regarding the use of revenue sharing funds at the local level were to an extent influenced by the uncertain and changing federal aid environment, and that beneficiaries of federal categorical grant programs which were reduced may have suffered from being caught in this intergovernmental cross fire.

Summary on Initial Impact

Diverse opinions as to the exact purpose of the General Revenue Sharing program existed in Washington at the time of the program's passage. This was no less true at the municipal level. In response to the question posed in the second survey, "Do you feel the purpose of

General Revenue Sharing was to bring about local tax relief or stimulate program spending?", thirty-eight local chief executives (53 percent) replied tax relief, while thirty-four (47 percent) thought it was meant to be stimulative.

Did the program meet the broadest goals implied—that it would rejuvenate the local decision-making process, produce a burst of creative energy, and allow local units of government to better identify and meet local needs? Clearly the decision-making processes of the cities surveyed here were not rejuvenated by the program's arrival. Decisions on the use of revenue sharing funds were made in the same manner as annual budgetary decisions. Comparing responses to Surveys I and II shows that local chief executives were able to predict sources of pressure as to uses of the funds fairly accurately; more importantly, the existence of community pressure, when it was experienced, did not have a great effect on the decisions ultimately made. The uses anticipated by local officials were the ones for the most part adopted. In response to the direct question, "Do you feel that revenue sharing has increased the city's ability to identify local needs?", a surprisingly honest 44 percent of local chief executives (thirty-six of eighty-two) said "no." One would think that, at least for good public relations, more would have answered differently.

Were local chief executives more creative in the use of revenue sharing funds compared to locally raised revenues? The dominant uses for capital improvements and local revenue substitution offer little evidence of that. Especially discouraging to those who hoped for dramatic impact was the increasing incidence of the maintain existing services use and concomitant decline in the new programs and expanded services categories over even the first two years of the program. The maintain use did little more than help hold the line, i.e., meet the increased cost of doing what was done by the city the year before. The fact that actual uses were not the same as local chief executive ideal uses shows that they were often influenced by factors other than their own perception of best use.

Since local chief executives in most cases could predict the uses to which the money was ultimately put, there was chief executive dominance of revenue sharing allocations that matches their role in traditional budgeting decisions. In California, especially, the extremely high rate of intrastate consensus as to the capital improvement use lends further support to the argument that the decisions were made based on program life, a calculus offered and reenforced in professional meetings and publications. One would expect variation in city characteristics and consequent need to produce much more diversity of use than found here. In New Jersey, local officials also appear at the mercy of an external variable, state tax structure, more than particularistic local conditions.

And if uncertainty influenced the initial use of revenue sharing monies for capital improvements, it also played a role in the decisions of local chief executives not to fund programs in areas traditionally supported by federal categorical grants. These survey results indicate that local governments intended to hold President Nixon to his promise that General Revenue Sharing was to provide them with new money, not to replace aid existing in other programs.

REVENUE SHARING AT TWELVE—THE 1984 SURVEY

How did the program's impact age? The same cities were surveyed in 1984 in an effort to gauge the continued impact of General Revenue Sharing. A 90 percent response rate was achieved.

In 71 percent of the cities responding, the decision-making process used to allocate revenue sharing funds was again not kept separate from the normal budgetary process. When asked if plans for use of revenue sharing funds were drawn up by the same individual who draws up the city budget, 76 percent responded in the affirmative. In terms of process, then, revenue sharing decisions were for the most part being handled, as expected, in the customary budgetary manner.

The 1984 data reveal for the first time an extremely high degree of consistency on uses between the two states. Revenue sharing allocations in 1984 showed a marked increase in the maintain existing services category in both states, now representing 68 percent of the first choices mentioned by chief executives overall and noted as at least one of the uses by 81 percent of the city executives (Table 3-17). The use of revenue sharing funds to maintain services jumped most dramatically in New Jersey since the 1974 survey (Table 3-8), suggesting that even reducing property taxes was becoming a luxury that cities in that state could not afford—only six cities indicated that use as the primary use. Capital improvement use was beyond the reach of New Jersey's cities, and while that use remained important in California, its priority rating dropped there, too. City officials there also noted a sharp increase since 1974 in the primary use of revenue sharing funds to maintain existing services.

Queries were again made of city chief executives in an effort to determine if uncertainty over the program's future were still encouraging the maintain and capital uses. They were asked again, as they had been in 1974, "If revenue sharing were to be discontinued, in what way would you allocate your last allocation?" The only responses noted by city chief executives were maintain and capital improvements—no other category received a single vote. When asked what the most valid

TABLE 3-17
1984 Uses—More Similarity Between States

California

Use	Mentioned	%	1st Choice	%
Maintain Services	44	70%	41	65%
Capital Improvements	29	46%	17	28%
Reduce Property Taxes	6	9%	2	3%
Initiate New Programs	8	13%	0	0%
Expand Existing Services	4	6%	1	1%
Other	1	1%	0	0%
	N = 63		N = 61	

New Jersey

Use	Mentioned	%	1st Choice	%
Maintain Services	24	89%	20	77%
Capital Improvements	6	22%	0	0%
Reduce Property Taxes	12	44%	6	23%
Initiate New Programs	3	11%	0	0%
Expand Existing Services	5	19%	0	0%
Other	0	0%	0	0%
	N = 27		N = 26	

criticism of the revenue sharing program was, "Program future is uncertain/hinders planning" surprisingly beat out "Cities do not get enough" as a very valid criticism by a margin of 52 percent to 39 percent (Table 3-18). Proving consistent, city officials indicated that their preferred reform of the program would be to have the "program made permanent," ranked first by 59 percent, while "more funds allocated" is a distant second at 23 percent (Table 3-19). City officials were clearly willing to trade certainty for dollars. These are very important findings.

There were reasons other than the desire to reduce the impact of potential program termination for the higher incidence in 1984 of the maintain existing services use. Inflation steadily eroded the value and therefore the impact of a program whose initial impact constituted approximately 5 percent of city budgets. It fell to about 3.5 percent by 1984, a small amount when considering the fact that municipal budgets had averaged 8 percent annual increases over the preceding ten years. For many cities, then, General Revenue Sharing had by 1984 most likely come to be treated as general revenue, albeit with an uncertainty factor attached. The Property Tax Revolt begun by California's Proposition 13 in 1978 had put fear of raising taxes into elected officials across the

TABLE 3-18
City Officials Like Program Uncertainty the Least

	Very Valid	%	Somewhat Valid	%	Not Valid	%
Money Goes to Cities Without Need	13	14%	45	50%	27	30%
Cities Do Not Get Enough	35	39%	37	41%	13	14%
Causes Wasteful Spending	2	22%	15	17%	68	76%
Reduces Local Autonomy	3	3%	23	26%	60	67%
Produces Loss of Accountability	1	1%	11	12%	70	78%
Program Future is Uncertain/ Hinders Planning	47	52%	38	42%	2	2%

$N = 90$

nation. When asked to characterize the impact of revenue sharing funds on the local property tax yield, 47 percent said it had prevented an increase or reduced the increase, in effect helping to maintain existing services.

Another reason for increased use of revenue sharing funds to help pay for ongoing programs or substitute for local revenue was the effect of spending and revenue limits on both California and New Jersey cities. New Jersey had enacted a local expenditure cap law, and California cities were subject to Proposition 13, which limited property tax revenue, and Proposition 4, which limited spending growth. City officials were asked, "Does the existence of a local tax/expenditure limit

TABLE 3-19
Making Program Permanent Is Most Popular Reform

	Mentioned	%	1st Choice	%
More Funds Allocated	69	77%	21	23%
Program Made Permanent	79	88%	53	59%
Index Program for Inflation	61	68%	8	9%
Tie To Set Percentage of Federal Revenues	25	28%	2	2%
Change Distribution Formula	17	19%	3	3%
Other	1	1%	0	0%

$N = 90$ $N = 90$

increase the tendency to use revenue sharing funds to do any of the following?" They were given the choices "substitute for local revenue," "allow for additional expenditures," or "no effect." Of the eighty-four responding, 70 percent stated the primary impact was to cause a substitution for local revenue, compared to only 18 percent who felt the result was an increased ability to provide additional expenditures— all of the latter in California. This suggests that the tax limitation was more effective than the expenditure constraint in California, and that the existence of an expenditure cap in New Jersey restrained any inclination to use revenue sharing funds to expand budgets and therefore increased their use to substitute for locally raised revenue.

By 1984, cutbacks in federal aid initiated by President Reagan provided an opportunity to again test the willingness of city officials to replace lost categorical or block grant money with revenue sharing funds. Chief executives in 68 percent of the cities (sixty-two cities) reported that their city had experienced some cutback in federal aid over the most recent two years, and 40 percent (twenty-six cities) said they had not replaced those funds. Only six chief executives said any revenue sharing funds were used for this purpose. When those who did not replace funds cut back by Washington were asked why they were not replaced, twenty-six cities noted a lack of local revenues available, ten said a desire to continue federal funding was the motivation (multiple responses were allowed), while none selected "program failure." If New Federalisms are intended to result in decentralized decisions which are actually based on the merits of previously federally funded programs, local revenue ability may be an important factor. There may also be a time lag as local governments psychologically withdraw from the targeted aid.

The response to one question summed up General Revenue Sharing at twelve. When asked, "Does General Revenue Sharing accomplish anything other than mild fiscal relief," 78 percent of chief executives responding admitted "no."

FINAL USES—THE 1988 SURVEY

City officials were always worried that the program would end, and it did. General Revenue Sharing was terminated in 1986, with the last distributions for the most part arriving at city halls for inclusion in the fiscal year 1987 budget. A survey was sent out in 1988 to the cities in the study to record the final uses of revenue-sharing funds. The response rate was 89 percent.

The survey asked city chief executives to comment on use of the last full allocation and the final allocation, which was a partial one. As Table 3-20 reveals, the use to maintain existing services remained strong

TABLE 3-20
1986 Uses—Final Full Allocation

California

Use	Mentioned	%	1st Choice	%
Maintain Services	38	58%	30	47%
Capital Improvements	36	55%	29	45%
Reduce Property Taxes	0	0%	0	0%
Initiate New Programs	7	11%	0	0%
Expand Existing Services	10	15%	3	5%
Other	4	6%	2	3%
	N = 66		N = 64	

New Jersey

Use	Mentioned	%	1st Choice	%
Maintain Services	17	80%	12	60%
Capital Improvements	0	0%	0	0%
Reduce Property Taxes	10	48%	6	30%
Initiate New Programs	2	10%	1	5%
Expand Existing Services	3	14%	0	0%
Other	1	5%	1	5%
	N = 20		N = 20	

in both states, hopefully minimizing the impact of termination, while California officials increased their use of the last full allocation for capital improvements. The two choices not surprisingly accounted for 85 percent of the first choice uses of the last full allocation. Since cities had increasingly made their spending decisions as if the program would end, they were prepared and spent the money in ways to minimize the effect of its loss on the next fiscal year. It was not a great loss; 78 percent of cities reported that revenue sharing had dwindled to less than 3 percent of their operating budget. But a loss it was. For some cities it meant a loss of millions of dollars, hundreds of thousands of dollars for others. All money is appreciated when revenue raising is constrained.

OTHER STUDIES

The major findings presented here have been confirmed by many other studies of the impact of General Revenue Sharing.

Most found that the process for allocation of revenue sharing funds to a great extent mirrored and in many cases overlapped the traditional budgeting practices. One study, by Timothy Almy, also found local chief executives to be firmly in control of the revenue sharing allocation process: "city manager preferences for spending are very significant predictors of actual allocations."[24] While disagreeing over the exact degree of community pressure and conflict surrounding the program's allocations, most studies agreed that there were no earthshaking changes from traditional budget deliberations. An NSF–RANN study, for example, noted that fewer than 40 percent of local governments held hearings on the first allocation, and fewer than 15 percent did so on the second round.[25] Where citizen participation through public hearings was documented, it was found to be inconsequential and to rapidly decline.[26] The NSF–RANN study also found that only about a third of chief executives found that the program made discovering community preferences, or setting priorities, easier.

With respect to actual uses of the funds, the NSF–RANN study as well as the Brookings monitoring project confirm this study's finding of a highly disproportionate use of revenue sharing funds for capital improvements.[27] Caputo and Cole reported that in the second year of the program, 48 percent of revenue sharing funds in the cities in their sample reportedly were used for capital improvement purposes.[28] Catherine Lovell studied ninety-seven southern California cities with similar results.[29] The U.S. Advisory Commission on Intergovernmental Relations documented the importance of uncertainty over the program's future and the resultant incentive to spend on capital improvements, as did NSF–RANN.[30]

The use of revenue sharing funds to maintain services and substitute for local taxes was also documented in the NSF–RANN and Brookings studies. The latter found that more than one-half of General Revenue Sharing appropriations to local governments took the place of taxes or borrowing.[31] Brookings field associates also found that cities with the most extreme fiscal pressure devoted a greater proportion of General Revenue Sharing to substitution than cities in better fiscal condition. By the second year of the program, Richard Nathan concluded that "there was a significant decline in the use of shared revenue for new spending. . ."[32] Caputo and Cole's survey also found that in 1973, 71 percent of revenue sharing was used for existing programs.[33]

Patrick Larkey conducted the most sophisticated statistical analysis of revenue sharing's early impact, modeling the expected expenditures for five cities and then comparing actual expenditures to those projected in an attempt to determine fiscal impact. He found that the more fiscal pressure there was, the more revenue sharing funds tended to be merged with other general operating funds and used to support existing expenditure obligations. When fiscal pressure was lower, the funds were more likely to be used for revenue displacement, the accumulation of a surplus, increased funding of basic services, and/or capital projects.[34] An analysis by the Kennedy School concluded that ". . . cities tend to use revenue sharing grants to lower their tax burdens, not to increase their service levels."[35]

Every study found public safety to be the leading functional area beneficiary of revenue sharing decisions at the local level. Caputo and Cole, for example, found 76 percent of the cities in their sample using revenue sharing funds for law enforcement purposes.[36] They also found, as here, that cities in Western states initially tended more than those in any other region to use funds for parks and recreation purposes. Finally, as in this study, observers found little of the funds being allocated to social services and/or to replace federal categorical cutbacks.[37] Richard Nathan testified before Congress that:

> . . . we found cases where state and local agencies and interest groups favoring certain programs threatened by proposed federal budget cuts decided not to press for shared revenue as a replacement because they were concerned that this would undermine the case they were making in Washington that particular grant-in-aid funds should be restored in the *federal* budget.[38]

Thus, while some variation naturally exists, the results of this study are supported by most of the other research projects on the impact of the General Revenue Sharing program on cities. Perhaps the only interesting variation here is the early and dominant use of revenue sharing funds in New Jersey cities for property tax reduction, a product of that state's state–local revenue system and a finding worthy on its own.

In sum, all available research suggests that it was difficult to find evidence of bursts of creative energy or innovative programs. A great majority of cities used the funds for capital improvement projects, to provide existing services, and/or to substitute for local tax revenue.

SUMMARY AND CONCLUSIONS

The leading hypothesis of this study was that neither the municipal budget process nor its outcomes would be greatly affected by the arrival of the new form of federal aid, revenue sharing. It was thought that as municipal budgeting was an executive-dominated, routinized, and generally insulated process, traditional roles and outcomes would be the rule and the type of impact hoped for by program sponsors the exception. The data confirmed the hypothesis. Results from the surveys show that the process for allocation of revenue sharing funds was initially a carbon copy of, and later indistinguishable from, customary budget practices.

The uses did not come close to matching the rhetoric from Washington. City executives neither expected nor reported actually using much of the new revenue to initiate new programs or expand existing services. While "creative" does not necessarily imply expansionary, it is apparent that city officials were driven by forces not related to the particular needs of their respective cities. The predominant early use in California cities for capital improvements was more a product of uncertainty over the program's future life expectancy than the need to rebuild earthquake-ravaged municipal buildings throughout the state, which the data in isolation might suggest. Even here there was little program stimulation: fifty of the fifty-two California cities responding to the 1974 question said the capital improvements had been previously planned, as opposed to developed upon receipt of the funds. In New Jersey the overall tax structure of the state, with a resultant over-reliance on the property tax, forced local executives to use nearly all of their early allocations for tax substitution purposes.

Both of these predominant uses benefited, as some had expected of a program of unrestricted aid, the great majority of city residents rather than any targeted population. The *New Republic*'s caution to those who thought that local use of revenue sharing funds would particularly benefit the poor—"There are far larger constituencies behind better street paving and larger police forces than behind welfare reform or compensatory education"—was realized.[39] Majoritarian politics dominated early use of revenue sharing funds.

By the second year of the program, uses in cities in both states moved toward the not very exciting maintain existing services use, for two reasons. Fear of program termination, however premature, overcame the tremendous diversity between the two states and the variety of circumstances of cities within each. It led city officials to add the actuarially-sound use of maintaining services to capital improvements, both areas where termination of revenue sharing would have the least negative fallout.

Meanwhile, as General Revenue Sharing was not actually tied to the growth in the federal income tax or indexed to inflation, its importance shrank over time as city budgets grew. With the cost of providing services rising faster than local revenues in many cites, revenue sharing funds provided a needed supplement to funding basic local services, but not much more. City officials would have liked to do more. In the 1984 survey, 78 percent of those responding to a question regarding their opinion as to their city's level of expenditure rated it "low" or "too low." Thirty chief executives rated inadequate tax revenue as their number one problem, the highest response. It ranked higher than unemployment, chosen by fifteen, and crime, selected by thirteen.

Characteristics of the program, then, hindered local creativity. Elected and appointed officials of beach, bedroom, and industrial park communities, with wildly varying socioeconomic profiles, were almost all driven by the same incentives to safe uses of revenue sharing funds. In the long run, economic theory was right; recipient governments would spend unrestricted aid in line with their normal priorities.

In fact, it is important to emphasize that the use of revenue sharing funds to help maintain local services should not necessarily be viewed negatively. Testimony of city officials had been warning since the program's passage of the increasing difficulty of financing basic services. Creativity must come in addition to the necessities, not in place of them. Further, the mere injection of some unrestricted aid from the federal government into the local revenue stream reduced, however slightly, the overall regressivity of the federal fiscal system, substituting to a great extent revenue from the progressive federal income tax revenues for those from the much more regressive property tax. Unfortunately, these had not been the predominant rationales for the program at passage.

The incremental impact of revenue sharing on cities is also found in the specific expenditure categories which were noted as benefiting from the funds. The three leading areas reported—public safety, public works, and parks and recreation—already make up the major municipal functions. Apparently local chief executives were taking no chances on this score either, refusing to give Washington a signal that they would pick up the slack for cutbacks in federal categorical or block grant programs. The unfortunate losers in this scenario may have been some program beneficiaries.

It could also be argued that local officials may have been too cautious. What makes for good intergovernmental politics, and what protects local officials from the politically difficult task of cutting programs or raising the revenues to continue them, may not have always been good policy. Revenue sharing could have provided seed money to try out ideas which otherwise might not have made it to the agenda, test them, and then determine their worth when measured against local resources. The "group-think" which resulted in cautious use of the funds, while understandable, may have prevented some good ideas (or even bad ones) from being tested, and ironically added fuel to the fire of opposition to revenue sharing.

Did revenue sharing make any difference at all to cities? It surely provided them with some important fiscal relief early in its existence, although that effect weakened over time. Local officials acted in a perfectly rational way, both managerially and politically. But ultimately this was not enough justification to have it continued.

NOTES

1. Of the fifty-eight California replies, forty-seven were signed by city managers, city administrators, or mayors, with the remainder completed by their assistants or department heads; of New Jersey's twenty-five responses, sixteen were signed by mayors, with the remainder again completed by assistants or department heads. This pattern was roughly repeated in the later surveys. The responses are a random sample of the total. There are no clear differences between those who did and did not reply.

2. In several cities, the responsibility was to be shared.

3. Throughout the survey, the total number of choices represented in tables will often be larger than the number of cities surveyed. This indicates that some local officials felt that more than one response was applicable.

4. "Revenue Sharing at Work in the Cities," *Public Management 55*, No. 1 (January 1973), p. 21.

5. Office of the Mayor, City and County of San Francisco, *General Revenue Sharing Preliminary Program*, mimeo, January 1973, p. 3.

6. United States Bureau of the Census, cited in Committee on Ways and Means, United States House of Representatives, Hearings, Parts 1–8, June 2–8, 1971 (Washington, DC: U.S. Government Printing Office, 1971).

7. Calculated from the U.S. Department of Commerce, Bureau of the Census, *Government Finances in 1972* (Washington, DC: U.S. Government Printing Office, 1973).

8. U.S. Advisory Commission on Intergovernmental Relations, *Measuring the Fiscal Capacity and Effort of State and Local Areas* (Washington, DC: U.S. Government Printing Office, 1971), pp. 126–127.

9. California city budget allocation data from State of California Controller, *Annual Report of Financial Transactions, California Cities*, FY 1970–71.

10. New Jersey city budget allocation data from State of New Jersey, Department of Community Affairs, *Local Government Expenditure Data*, FY 1970–71.

11. Office of the Mayor, City and County of San Francisco, *General Revenue Sharing*, p. 3.

12. See Crecine, *Government Problem Solving*.

13. Crecine, *Government Problem Solving*, p. 191. It should also be noted that an analysis of the impact of union pressure activity on use of revenue-sharing funds was not conducted due to the small number of cities reporting such activity.

14. Richard Nathan in *Revenue Sharing*, Hearings Before the Subcommittee on Intergovernmental Relations of the Committee on Government Operations,

U.S. House, Ninety-third Congress, Second Session, Part I (Washington, DC: U.S. Government Printing Office, 1975), p. 318.

15. Moon Landrieu in *General Revenue Sharing*, Hearings Before the Subcommittee on Revenue Sharing of the Committee on Finance, U.S. Senate, Ninety-Fourth Congress, First Session (Washington, DC: U.S. Government Printing Office, 1975), p. 318.

16. Again, see David O. Sears and Jack Citrin, *The Property Tax Revolt.*

17. Meltsner and Wildavsky, "Leave City Budgeting Alone!", p. 326.

18. Nathan, *Revenue Sharing*, p. 427.

19. Kenneth Gibson, in Hearings Before the Subcommittee on Intergovernmental Relations, p. 533.

20. Gibson, Hearing Before the Subcommittee, pp. 533–534.

21. Further, we would not expect chief executives to report general government expenditures as frequently as the more service-oriented program categories.

22. See, again, Deil Wright, *Understanding Intergovernmental Relations,* and Jeffrey Pressman, *Federal Programs and City Politics.*

23. Jeffrey Pressman, "Political Implications of the New Federalism," in Wallace Oates, ed., *Financing the New Federalism*, pp. 277–281.

24. Timothy A. Almy, "City Managers, Public Avoidance, and Revenue Sharing," *Public Administration Review* 37 (January/February 1977), p. 26.

25. Thomas J. Anton and Richard Hofferbert, "Assessing the Political Impact of General Revenue Sharing: Local Perspectives," Institute for Social Research, Preliminary Report No. 2 for NSF–RANN Study, University of Michigan, Ann Arbor, Michigan, February 28, 1975.

26. Richard L. Cole and David A. Caputo, "The Public Hearing as an Effective Citizen Participation Mechanism: A Case Study of the General Revenue Sharing Program," *American Political Science Review* 78 (1984): 404–416.

27. See Cole and Caputo, "The Public Hearing," and Richard P. Nathan, Allen D. Manvel, and Susannah E. Calkins, *Monitoring Revenue Sharing* (Washington, DC: Brookings, 1975).

28. David Caputo and Richard Cole, "General Revenue Sharing Decisions in Cities Over 50,000," *Public Administration Review*, March/April 1975, p. 136.

29. Catherine Lovell, "Implementation of Conflicting Goals," paper presented at 1976 Annual Meeting of the Western Political Science Association, San Francisco, April 1–3, 1976. See also Lovell, "General Revenue Sharing and Categorical Grants: Comparative Effects on Selected California Cities," in *General Revenue Sharing and Decentralization*, ed. Walter F. Scheffer (Norman, OK: University of Oklahoma Press, 1976): 115–166.

30. U.S. Advisory Commission on Intergovernmental Relations, "Revenue Sharing: View from the Field," *Information Bulletin* No. 73–3, March 1973.

31. Nathan in Subcommittee on Revenue Sharing, Hearings, p. 154.

32. Nathan et al., *Monitoring Revenue Sharing.*

33. See Caputo and Cole, "General Revenue Sharing Decisions."

34. See Patrick Larkey, *Evaluating Public Programs.*

35. Helen F. Ladd and John Yinger, et al., *The Changing Economic and Fiscal Conditions of Cities*, Draft Final Report prepared for the U.S. Department of Housing and Urban Development, Grant No. HC5655 (July 1985), p. 13–11.

36. Caputo and Cole, *General Revenue Sharing Decisions.* See also Kathryn Newcomer and Susan Welch, "The Impact of General Revenue Sharing on Spending in Fifty Cities," *Urban Affairs Quarterly* 18, No. 1 (1982): 131–144.

37. On social services, see *National Journal*, op. cit., pp. 1102–1103. On federal aid, see "Few Cities Use U.S. Windfall to Save Poverty Programs," *Christian Science Monitor*, April 14, 1973, p. 1.

38. Before the Subcommittee on Intergovernmental Relations, Hearings, p. 445.

39. "Revenue Sharing that Works," *The New Republic* 164, No. 22, May 29, 1971, p. 8.

4

Between the Idea and the Reality: General Revenue Sharing Is Terminated

On November 30, 1983, President Ronald Reagan signed the Local Government Fiscal Assistance Amendments of 1983, which continued General Revenue Sharing for local governments, stating, "The Federal Government never spent money more wisely than by devoting it to general revenue sharing."[1] Three years later the program expired. As had been true at its passage, there were wildly varying reactions: some were shocked at its demise, while others were amazed that it had lasted as long as it had.

General Revenue Sharing ostensibly became a victim of federal deficit reduction, which by the mid-1980s had become *the* most pressing domestic policy issue. But while the program may not have lived up to the most optimistic goals of its sponsors, other underachieving programs survived the deficit-cutting movement. There were clearly other factors at work, including changes over the life of revenue sharing in the way congressional campaigns were run with a resultant decline in the influence of state and local officials, and an intellectual stampede toward public choice theory and its belief in competition between governments. This chapter will review the earlier legislative actions regarding revenue sharing before presenting and analyzing the debate on its ultimate demise.

THE 1976 REAUTHORIZATION: SOME LOOSENING, SOME TIGHTENING

While the General Revenue Sharing program was reauthorized in 1976 and 1980, and in 1983 for local governments, the debates at each stage, along with some changes in program requirements, laid the groundwork for its termination.

On April 25, 1975, President Gerald Ford proposed legislation reauthorizing General Revenue Sharing for five and three-quarters years, through fiscal 1982.[2] General support for the program in Congress was strong, even stronger than it had been at its passage, although there were pockets of criticism on both the left and right.

In somewhat of a turnaround from the initial debates over the program, liberals expressed the most concerns, including issues involving the distribution formula, general uses of the funds, enforcement of the antidiscrimination provision, and the lack of public participation.[3] Three members of the subcommittee with jurisdiction over the program, the Intergovernmental Relations Subcommittee of the House Government Operations Committee, were particularly critical. It was reported that Barbara Jordan (D-TX), John Burton (D-CA), and Robert Drinan (D-MA) found that the program failed "... to do enough for poor people, minorities and cities with the worst urban problems."[4]

The complaint over the distribution formula had been aired by Wilbur Mills (D-AR) and others during the debate over passage, and most basically was an objection to the fact that federal money went to rich local governments at all, while not enough was distributed to those which were poor. This revived the broader question over the purpose of revenue sharing: was it to remedy horizontal fiscal imbalance, and thus be redistributive as liberals preferred, or was its purpose to reinvigorate *all* state and local governments by sharing federal revenues? Related to this was the effect of ceilings and floors in the formula, meant to ensure that no per capita allocation to a county or individual city or township could be more than 145 percent of the statewide per capita distribution, keeping the poorer places from getting *too* much, or that no city or township's allocation would be less than 20 percent of that same figure, ensuring that everyone, whether needy or not, benefited.

There were also critics of the uses of the funds. Commenting on what were the same predominant local uses of revenue sharing found in this study,

> Congressional liberals and civil rights and public interest groups have focused much of their criticism on the ways local governments have spent their revenue sharing dollars. They have complained that governments have devoted too much funding to capital projects or tax cuts benefiting the affluent and too little to social programs aiding the poor, elderly or minorities.[5]

A GAO survey of twenty-two local governments found that through June 30, 1974, only 3 percent of revenue-sharing funds had been allocated to social services for the poor or elderly, a finding supported here and in a report by the liberal National Clearinghouse on Revenue Sharing.

Public interest and civil rights groups further claimed that the antidiscrimination provision of the legislation was being poorly enforced. The National Clearinghouse claimed to have documented widespread discrimination, and particularly faulted the designation of the Office of Revenue Sharing in the Treasury Department as the unit of government responsible for enforcing the prohibition. Some thought that the Justice Department, with more experience in this area, would be the better choice.

Finally, there were those who bemoaned the lack of public participation in the local decision-making processes regarding the use of revenue-sharing funds. As in this study, the GAO report found that the program had no measurable impact on participation. Those concerned wanted to strengthen requirements for citizen involvement.

Fiscal conservatives offered objections familiar from the struggle over passage, including the separation of taxing and spending decisions, and the lack of congressional control over the funds. Rep. Jack Brooks of Texas, chair of the House Government Operations Committee, while agreeing with some of the liberal criticism, also questioned the program's philosophy:

> ... greater accountability to the people is achieved through a system designed to require those who propose various spending projects to also levy the taxes necessary to support the projects.[6]

In a boding of things to come, Brooks also expressed concern over the growing federal deficit and suggested he would consider recommending that the program be subject to annual appropriations, a grave concern for the state and local lobby.

There were important discussions and disagreements within the House Subcommittee on Intergovernmental Relations, and ultimately different bills were offered on the House floor by the full committee and its subcommittee. Of particular note in the subcommittee were discussions over the appropriations issue and the distribution formula. The subcommittee voted by a narrow margin (7–6) to authorize but not automatically appropriate funds for the program. Opponents of revenue sharing contended it should not take priority over other programs competing for federal funds. By a fairly wide margin (10–1) the subcommittee voted to retain in the formula the use of per capita income as a measure of need.

Some members of the full committee had let it be known that they favored substituting the number of persons below the poverty line, which would make the program more redistributive. Finally, there was an Administration-backed attempt to raise the ceiling local governments could receive from 145 percent of the state's per capita grant to 175 percent, again to target funds to more needy places. The motion lost 7–5.[7] The state and local coalition was seen as fragile when it came to formula changes, as they had the potential to undo the base of support for revenue sharing. One of the White House's legislative staff said that changing the way allocations were made would "without a doubt" result in political trouble for revenue sharing.[8] Indeed, after the U.S. Conference of Mayors broke with the other state–local interest groups to support changes in the formula, the *National Journal* asked, "Is the Revenue Sharing Lobby Coming Unstrung?"[9]

On the floor of the House, Subcommittee Chair L.H. Fountain (D-NC) offered a successful amendment which deleted three additions the full Committee had made: a new formula to distribute an extra $150 million per year based on need, using the poverty line measure; a requirement that state governments submit an annual report on efforts aimed at modernizing state and local government; and an expansion of the Davis–Bacon Act to cover all projects using any revenue sharing funds, as opposed to the existing requirement applying it when 25 percent of the project used the federal aid.

It also substituted the subcommittee's civil rights provisions for those of the full Committee, which some had worried could deny local governments due process and which were generally seen as too burdensome. The broadest criticism of the full Committee's version was that it could impose "unbearable restrictions" on local governments, increasing administrative costs, counter to the general philosophy of revenue sharing.[10] The Subcommittee's substitute measure passed 233–172, the nay votes yielding evidence of the desire of many members of the House to regain some control over revenue sharing and thus opening a chink in its armor.

The appropriations issue was brought up on the floor, with (not surprisingly) Appropriations Committee members and Budget Committee Chair Brock Adams (D-WA) trying to subject the program to the annual appropriations process beginning in fiscal 1979. Adams said, foreshadowing later developments:

> Revenue sharing happens to be the biggest and worst of the back-door spending programs we have. . . . If we ever want to control the federal budget of the United States, we are going to have to reduce these mandatory programs and put them under the control of the authorizing committees and appropriations committees on a regularized basis. . . . I am simply saying it is a matter of fiscal control.[11]

A telegram helped to turn the tide. Democratic Governor Patrick Lucy of Wisconsin wrote to remind Congress that nineteen states, like his, had biennial budget processes and needed to be assured of the funds for at least two years in making their budget decisions. The move to subject revenue sharing to annual appropriations failed, 150–244, but again the armor was nicked. Also of note was an early flexing of what later would be extremely important senior citizen power, as the House by voice vote passed an amendment to try to assure seniors a voice in local hearings over use of the funds.

The final vote on HR 13367 was 361–35, reflecting the strong overall support for the program. Importantly, it eliminated the requirements that funds be spent for the designated priority uses and the prohibition on using revenue sharing funds as matching funds for federal grants. Both of these had been found to be unenforceable due to the "fungibility factor," i.e., the ability of local governments to substitute revenue-sharing money for local funds.

There was less dissension in the Senate Finance Committee than there had been in the House Government Operations Committee. It reported a bill with a 14–0 vote. The report accompanying the bill reaffirmed the original rationale for revenue sharing:

> By providing federal funds with few limitations, the committee believes that state and local governments may more effectively meet the diverse needs and priorities of the nation.[12]

It also highlighted the fiscal pressure on state and local governments:

> Rapidly rising service costs coupled with sluggish or declining tax bases has meant that state and local governments have had to raise tax rates and/or cut local services. . . . the committee concluded that state and local governments face financial problems of a continued severe nature.[13]

In hearings, the mayor of Newark, New Jersey, Kenneth Gibson, had underscored the problem for cities:

> Yet the delivery of basic services still remains the major responsibility of city government. And, while categorical programs have provided outside funds—mostly Federal funds—to help the cost of additional services, the Federal Government has continued under the assumption that cities could continue to afford the cost of basic services simply because we were already paying for them.
>
> If this were once true, it is no longer so. The cost of maintaining basic services has risen incredibly. The major portion of these costs is in

personnel. More than three-quarters of Newark's operating budget pays the salaries of our policemen, firemen, teachers, and sanitationmen.[14]

The committee suggested annual increases of $150 million in the amount of money shared to at least partly account for inflation. The committee had noted that annual payments to local governments rose by 25.5 percent over the five years of the program, while the consumer price index rose by 35 percent.

The full Senate increased that $150 million to $200 million. Among the other interesting issues raised on the floor of the Senate was the annual appropriations issue, which lost by a larger margin (14–62) than in the House. Senator Joseph Biden (D-DE), also a member of the Budget Committee, rather forcefully made the argument for it:

> We all know that control of our budgets, control of our spending, control of our government is one key to helping guide our economy, our employment, our inflation. Today we propose to throw away a $42 billion key to our country's well-being.[15]

There was also an amendment proposed which would have tied the amount of revenue sharing funds each year to federal income tax collections. Its sponsor, Senator James McClure (R-ID), thought it would make the program more fiscally responsible. It was defeated (7–70), ironically on the grounds that it would cause too much uncertainty for local governments and hurt them at the worst possible time, during a recession. There is no record of the position of state and local governments on this proposed change, which might actually have been to their great benefit in terms of both annual growth and program longevity. The Senate also added prohibitions against discrimination based on age, handicapped status, and religion.

The Senate passed the reauthorization of General Revenue Sharing by the overwhelming vote of 80–4. Senator Robert Packwood (R-OR) intoned:

> In my view, local governments spend money more wisely, spend it more cheaply and spend it more honestly than the federal government. The biggest favor the federal government can do for states, counties, for cities and for townships is to collect the money with the federal income tax, the federal corporation tax, and give it to local governments with as few strings as possible, not in hope but in the knowledge that they will spend it for their needs better than we could ever possibly spend it for their needs if we dictate how that money is to be spent from Washington, DC.[16]

The Senate also removed the "priority use" restriction on local governments and the ban on use of the funds to match federal grants. It went further than the House in eliminating the necessity of filing actual and planned use reports, saying they had been uninformative and were burdensome. The Senate hoped that by adding a citizen participation requirement necessary oversight would be provided at the local level, again in the spirit of the program.

Major differences ironed out by the House–Senate Conference committee included agreeing to extend the program three and three-quarters years, the House's version, as opposed to the five and three-quarters years approved by the Senate. The Senate got its $200 million add-on, but only for one year, fiscal 1978. The requirement that recipient governments file use reports was retained, and public hearings and local publication of information were newly required. The House approved the final version by a vote of 292–111, and the Senate followed by 77–4.

President Gerald Ford eagerly signed the measure. To prod Congress, he had already threatened to withhold his signature from two important bills, one appropriating funds for public works projects and one extending the emergency service jobs programs, until revenue sharing was passed.

In this first reauthorization, then, there was a strong reaffirmation of the concept of revenue sharing, but not without some nibbling at the margins. There was a lot of "good news—bad news:"

- the program was reauthorized for three and three-quarters years, but this was less than both the White House and Senate wanted, obviously indicating a lack of long-term support;
- similarly, there was an "inflation adjustment" of $200 million per year, but it was limited to only one year;
- attempts to subject revenue sharing to annual appropriations failed, but the issue was debated enough to remind everyone of the importance of controlling spending, and it allowed concern for deficits to creep into the discussion;
- there was discussion of the need to make the formula more redistributive, to send more aid to needier cities, but this too failed, explicitly weakening the rationale that the program was aimed at horizontal fiscal imbalance;
- the elimination of "high priority spending areas" for local governments would make complying easier, but also took away the veil of any national purpose being served by the funds. Without the redistributive rationale, it left some to ponder just what the purpose of revenue sharing was;
- the state and local lobby was strong, termed "the old general-revenue sharing steamroller" by one congressional aide, but

showed its long-term weakness by resisting any changes in the formula, however justifiable.

From the local government point of view, the new civil rights requirements could be burdensome. Receipt of revenue sharing funds opened many local governments to federal government regulation they had not previously experienced.[17] Some governments turned down their revenue sharing funds rather than be subject to provisions like these. Stoutsville, MO, turned its $222 check back in "with a letter telling the federal government to keep its nose out of Stoutsville's business."[18]

The newly mandated requirements for public participation also posed a threat to the program, not so much due to the cost of conducting them, but in the possibility (likelihood) that lack of success would become another criticism of the program. Expectations were once again raised. Social scientists had already been documenting the lack of political participation in cities.[19]

And President Ford's rhetoric, in building on the anti-Washington themes of Richard Nixon, fanned the flames of devolution which would ultimately result in the federal government greatly reducing aid to state and local governments, including revenue sharing:

> . . . the federal bureaucracy has grown and grown. Power inevitably is drawn away from your States, your counties, your cities, your towns to an increasingly centralized national Government—always bigger, always more meddlesome—but not always more efficient or more responsive to local needs.[20]

In sum, state and local governments may have won this General Revenue Sharing battle, but at the tender age of four the program had taken enough hits to make the war for long-term survival less assured.

THE 1980 REAUTHORIZATION: THE STATES LOSE THEIR SHARE

General Revenue Sharing was due to expire on September 30, 1980. President Jimmy Carter's budget proposal in January of that year included support for renewing General Revenue Sharing at previous levels. But on April 16 he delivered legislation to Congress which altered his original proposal. Carter reasoned:

> Since that time, inflation has accelerated considerably and it has become imperative that we restrain Federal spending and balance the federal budget.

> I therefore am proposing today that the revenue sharing program be extended only for local governments. I also am recommending that funding for the program be reduced to the transitional level of $5.1 billion in the next two fiscal years, and $4.6 billion in fiscal years 1983 through 1985.[21]

The first serious threat to revenue sharing's existence was now on the table.[22]

The state of the economy, then, and particularly an inflation rate which was approaching 14 percent, led President Carter to turn his back on the governors, his former colleagues. This was particularly interesting and informative in that 1980 was an election year, and one would assume that this action might weaken his support among them. As the termination of one $2.3 billion program was not likely to have that much of an impact on inflation and thus bring great political credit nationally, it can be assumed that Carter realized that campaign support from governors was no longer as important in a presidential campaign as it once had been.

To justify his proposed course of action, Carter also pointed to the improved fiscal situation of state governments.

> Most State governments are stronger fiscally than they were just a decade ago. They have broader and more responsive tax systems, which have produced rapid growth in revenues. In the last decade alone, State government revenues have grown sixty percent faster than the Gross National Product. Some States, as a result, have accumulated substantial budget surpluses.[23]

By being fiscally responsible, States had ironically put themselves in the position of losing support from a federal government that was becoming increasingly fiscally irresponsible.

In his message, Carter was clear to underscore the need to continue revenue sharing support for local governments.

> While the fiscal condition of the States has improved substantially, many local governments continue to have difficulty financing essential services with their own tax resources. These cities, counties, and towns are squeezed between the growing demands for services and shrinking tax bases. This fiscal squeeze is particularly severe for the cities and counties with large numbers of poor or disadvantaged citizens.[24]

Carter also proposed changes in the intrastate allocation formula to try to direct more of the funds to those local governments with the greatest need.

Under the existing formula, a poor city or town located in a rich county suffered, since the funds were first allocated at the county level. To remedy this reduction in the redistributive effect of revenue sharing, the Carter Administration proposed eliminating the use of county area as an allocation point, with all local governments obtaining their share on a statewide basis. They also recommended raising the maximum which could be received from 145 to 175 percent of the statewide per capita average. There were other formula changes offered to remedy, for example, the receipt of funds by high-income communities and the unjustifiably large allocations to localities whose high tax effort was actually the result of taxes exported to citizens outside those jurisdictions, most often through "tourist taxes" or taxes on minerals such as oil.

Recognizing that the response of state governments to the loss of revenue sharing funds would likely be a lessening of financial support of local governments, President Carter also proposed adding $500 million for local governments for two transitional years. Lobbyist Martin of the Governors Association saw this as a "divide the opposition" strategy, an attempt to buy local government silence in the debate on state share.[25] Carter also proposed extending the program for five years for local governments, with continued entitlement status.

The battle line was drawn. The debate on whether to eliminate state participation was laid out in a pro and con discussion in the *Congressional Digest* of June 7, 1980. Revenue sharing's longest and most ardent foe, Congressman Jack Brooks (D-TX), repeated his argument that first and foremost there was no revenue to share:

> When it was first conceived in the early 1960s, there may have been some logic to the idea of revenue sharing: the Federal government's revenue-raising resources were much greater and more efficient than those of State and local governments, and whenever they produced a surplus, those extra dollars should be returned to the States and communities.
>
> But by the time the Nixon Administration was able to sell this idea to Congress in 1972, the logic had already been demolished. Instead of a budget surplus, there was a deficit of nearly $30 billion that year, and the red ink has continued to flow ever since. We had a national debt of $437 billion in 1972. This year it is expected to come close to $900 billion, and a trillion-dollar debt—if you can conceive of such a number—is only a matter of time unless we cut out wasteful, unnecessary Federal spending.[26]

Brooks also pointed to the need to control inflation, the improved revenue systems of state and local governments and resultant strong state fiscal positions, and the doubling of federal aid to state and local governments between 1972 and 1979. In his conclusion, Brooks also reminded his audience of the "need" issue and lack of congressional control over use of the funds:

> The point is that mailing out money from the Federal treasury to State and local governments, without any regard for whether they need it or not or any control over how it is spent, is not a proper pastime for the Federal Government.[27]

He had recently called the program "a snake."[28]

While Brooks made no mention of retaining revenue sharing for local governments, another proponent of eliminating the state share, Rep. Richard Gebhart (D-MO), did:

> Local governments are not in the same position. Most do not have the taxing powers States have acquired in the past eight years. Many, particularly older industrial cities, are in dire financial straits facing threats of bankruptcy.[29]

Senator Cranston (D-CA) concurred:

> Unlike local governments, the states have full taxing powers. Their needs can be met in ways far more equitable than by increasing property taxes— the primary source of local government revenue.[30]

In arguing for retaining the states, Congressman John Wydler (D-NY) had an interesting retort to the state surplus argument. "Some say we should eliminate the States because some States have had large surplus balances. Along that line of reasoning, one might further inquire why State governments should be eligible for any Federal programs."[31]

In airing this view, Rep. Wydler highlighted that it is congressional desire for control over and credit for federal aid programs which makes categorical grant programs more popular in Washington than revenue sharing. He highlighted the inconsistency between recognizing the rising anti-big-government sentiment and doing away with part of a program aimed at bringing decisions closer to the people:

> With the current nationwide resentment against big government, one might wonder why the revenue sharing program is subject to such heated attack from some in Congress. The answer is simple: Revenue sharing stands for the proposition that all wisdom does not necessarily reside in Washington; that perhaps State and local officials, being closer to the situation, can better determine ways to solve local problems; that Washington does not always know best.[32]

The U.S. Advisory Commission on Intergovernmental Relations (ACIR) also thought that other programs should be cut before revenue sharing, pointing out its strengths in periods of fiscal austerity, including its flexibility "without the stimulative effects and high administrative costs of many other Federal aids."[33]

The Commission also made the very interesting point that, since state and local governments could use the funds as they wished and determining exact uses of the funds was almost impossible, in cutting revenue sharing Congress wouldn't know what they were actually cutting. The cuts would thus be arbitrary. "In contrast, if Congress decides that the Federal aid system must be a source of specific budget cuts, it can make a rational decision about what national priorities are."[34] The ACIR also reminded Congress that eliminating the state share would likely result in reduced state aid to local governments, and also raised the horizontal imbalance point that not all states would be equally able to absorb the cut. And, in noting that "The new fiscal strength of the States is largely traceable to courageous tax action by governors and State legislators in the mid-1960s and early 70s," the Commission may have not only implied that states should not be punished for their responsible fiscal behavior, but that perhaps Congress should show a little more courage on budget balancing themselves.

The National Governors Association again brought up the issue of the need for revenue sharing funds to meet unfunded federal government mandates, pointing out that one thousand of the twelve hundred mandates in existence in 1980 had been passed since the passage of revenue sharing.[35] And the National Conference of State Legislatures highlighted the particular importance of revenue sharing in a recession, which economists at the time were accurately predicting was just around the corner. Forcing states to raise taxes or cut spending during a recession would not be good fiscal policy.

In any case, a new dynamic was to be at work, one detected by James Howell and George Brown in 1979:

> Another problem which revenue sharing will encounter in the Congress is the increasing awareness of "trade-offs." In the past grant programs up for reauthorization were considered ostensibly on their own merits: Was a particular program achieving to a reasonable degree the congressional objectives? Now, however, there are attempts to contrast the benefits to be derived from one program to the potential benefits which the same sum of federal dollars might achieve in another area.[36]

In tight fiscal times, being successful would not necessarily be sufficient for budget success.

The battle in Congress was not as fiercely fought as one might have expected. In fact, members dragged their feet until the last minute, going beyond the expiration date for General Revenue Sharing before coming to a decision. As in previous debates over the program, most of the action was in the House.

While the Subcommittee of Intergovernmental Relations was working on the Administration's bill, which included removal of the states from the program, two attempts were made on the House floor to retain state participation. By the close vote of 192–225, the House defeated Rep. Barber Conable's (R-NY) proposal to have Congress cut categorical grants by 5 percent to provide funds necessary to retain the states. A proposal by Rep. James Quillen (R-OH), which would have cut science funds, foreign aid, and government overhead to fund GRS, lost 146–271. Congress clearly found cutting the unrestricted funds an easier political task than targeting and thus taking responsibility for specific cuts. Rep. Clarence Brown (R-OH) chastised his colleagues: "Hell hath no fury like a vested interest masquerading as a moral principle."[37] Governor Lee Dreyfus of Wisconsin recognized the dynamics:

> Congress will cut where it gets the least screaming, and there are only 50 voices—the state governors—interested in preserving [the state share of] general revenue sharing.[38]

Meanwhile, the subcommittee first agreed to put the States back in the program after one year, before reversing themselves on the last day of markup and cutting the states entirely. The full committee, Government Operations, disagreed, passing by a vote of 21–15 Congressman Ted Weiss's (D-NY) amendment to bring the states back in for fiscal 1982 and 1983, but only if the Appropriations Committee agreed to add the $2.3 billion each year. This certainly dismayed Committee Chair Brooks, who said, to avoid all uncertainty as to his view, "I would like to bury this bill and collect what we've already handed out—we could call it deficit sharing."[39] The subcommittee also had reduced the reauthorization from the White House-backed five years to three, cut the $500 million a year which had been proposed as transitional funds for local governments, and, in proving the adage that "a good formula is an old formula," refused to accept any of the administration's proposed formula changes.

A month later, the full committee reversed its decision and by a 20–15 vote took the states out for good. The committee did agree to an antirecession program which could send $1 billion a year to state and local governments should a recession occur. They also defeated a proposal by Rep. Weiss to give local governments an extra allocation of 40 percent of the $2.3 billion being cut for states, the amount of state revenue sharing funds estimated to be passed along to local governments in state aid.

The Senate Finance Committee, perhaps reflecting the fact that the Senate is supposed to represent states, voted 11–7 to include States for 1982–1985, after having them sit out 1981. But it subjected the state portion to discretionary appropriation. It retained entitlement status for local governments and extended the program for five years, two more than committee action in the House. They also approved the countercyclical revenue-sharing plan.

General Revenue Sharing formally expired on September 30, but Congress knew it had more time since the next payments were not due to go out until January 1981. While some mounted a fight on the House floor to restore the states, others, moving in the other direction, wanted to take the entitlement status away from local governments. Rep. Jim Mattox (D-TX) took the latter position: "If revenue sharing requires an appropriation, then I'll have another shot at killing that sucker off."[40]

The bill which was ultimately passed by the House allowed everyone to get a little of what they wanted, but for the States it was ultimately not enough. By a 345–21 vote, an overwhelming display of support in difficult budget times, the house continued the $4.6 billion in annual allotments to local governments for three years and retained its entitlement status. By adopting on a 255–118 vote an amendment by Rep. Wydler, it also included $2.3 billion for states, but those funds would be subject to annual appropriations, the first nail in the coffin. This amendment also did away with the countercyclical funds. Budget Committee Chairman Robert Giaimo (D-CT) referred to the recent election of Ronald Reagan: "Last week there was an overwhelming mandate—the commitment and insistence of the American people is clearly enunciated—get control of federal spending."[41]

Also damaging was a provision which was then agreed to by voice vote, requiring that each state government make a choice between revenue sharing funds and categorical grants. States would have to give back or turn down a dollar of categorical aid for every dollar in revenue-sharing funds it received. Rep. Elliott Levitas, who offered the amendment, said:

> For every dollar that a categorical program is disavowed by a state because they do not want it and do not need it, to that extent they will receive general revenue sharing money to spend as they so desire. It does it without adding to the budget, without adding to the deficit.[42]

Congress was calling the states' bluff that revenue sharing was "the most important federal aid program."

Because it was getting so late in the session, the Senate took the unusual move of working from the House-passed version, and on December 9 passed by a vote of 80–3 a revenue sharing extension for five years, which also included funding for states in fiscal years 1982 and 1983.

The House avoided a conference by calling up a resolution which accepted certain Senate-passed provisions, while rejecting others. It passed by 337–19. The Senate went along by a voice vote on December 12 when, in fear of having the reauthorization bill die at adjournment, it capitulated to the major House demands. The reauthorization included the states in fiscal 1982 and 1983, but only after Appropriations Committee action, and only for states which were willing to trade categorical dollars for revenue sharing funds—in effect, stopping their participation. The program was extended for the three years the House had wanted, versus the five sought by the White House and the Senate.

At eight years of age, then, General Revenue Sharing faced a midlife crisis, its identity increasingly adrift. The deficit had now been forcefully used as an argument for terminating the state share of revenue sharing, and many felt that despite the wide margin in favor of reauthorization for local governments, their time would come too.

There were several interesting occurrences during this renewal. The States didn't fight as hard as many thought they would. Why? The revenue-sharing allocation of 1980 amounted to only about 1.2 percent of state general revenue, "small money" according to National Governors Association lobbyist Jim Martin.[43] States were also guilty as charged of being in sound fiscal shape, at least in the aggregate, and this prosperity may have taken some of the fight out of them. Aggregate state balances, calculated as the difference between total general expenditures and total general revenues as a percentage of total general revenues, were 3.5 percent of general expenditures for fiscal 1980, as opposed to the −8.5 percent when revenue sharing was passed in 1972 and −6.2 percent at its 1976 reauthorization.[44]

The targeting of the state share for extinction also weakened the state–local lobbying coalition. The National League of Cities, for example, was silent on the issue in the early stages of the debate. The head of the league's federal relations "said the group was not lobbying at all on revenue sharing because the local governments retained their funds and all the league is concerned with is protecting the local share."[45] This may have been shortsighted, as it did not go unnoticed by the governors, according to Martin. When the local share was later threatened, the state lobby groups for the most part stayed at home. The *National Journal* had warned:

> The cutoff of the state share could, however, have profound implications for intergovernmental lobbying efforts in Washington. The state, county and city lobbying groups would lose the symbol of unity around which they have built a powerful, broad-based coalition that affects an array of federal programs. Lobbyists for these groups also fear that the loss of the states' revenue sharing may be just the opening wedge of efforts to reduce many forms of federal grants in times of severe inflation, national budgetary strain and balanced budget pressures in Washington.[46]

This would turn out to be very prophetic.

The confusion surrounding the overall purpose of General Revenue Sharing is also evident throughout this debate over reauthorization. State use of the funds, other than as aid to local governments, was hardly mentioned in Congress. In fact, several of the comments on the local government share seemed to accept the use of revenue sharing funds for basic services in hard-pressed cities. Since innovative uses no longer seemed to be the accepted rationale for the program, one would expect that it would be better targeted to compensate for horizontal fiscal imbalances. This position was taken in the Administration proposal and by some members of Congress, but never got very far; when a program becomes more redistributive, it inherently loses support. Overall, then, the purpose of revenue sharing was becoming less clear.

Congress had came up with the interesting tactic of offering states revenue sharing dollars for categorical dollars turned back. On the one hand, this could be seen as calling the states' bluff that revenue sharing was, from their perspective, the best federal aid program. But for states, while revenue sharing may have been the best program from a policy point of view, cutting categorical grant programs would be worse politically. These programs are more directly and visibly targeted to specific individuals or groups; cutting them would produce more of an outcry and political backlash than cutting revenue sharing, with benefits less obviously targeted. Congress was, in effect, asking the states to do what it had not been willing to do itself—it was indeed offering deficit sharing. Members surely knew that states would not, could not take this deal. But Congress could then also take the position that it didn't really cut the state share of General Revenue Sharing.

State leaders had also made a tactical mistake, angering Congress by calling, in nearly thirty states, for a constitutional amendment to balance the federal budget. This would give revenue sharing opponents like Senator Birch Bayh the opportunity to chastise them: "I find it the ultimate hypocrisy for state legislators to tell us to balance the budget, but don't cut funds to the states."[47]

Finally, the debate over reauthorization showed that the choir of deficit-reduction hawks was growing, as this was certainly the main reason offered for cutting off states. While revenue sharing had been proclaimed "an idea whose time has come" in 1972, deficit reduction seemed to be the idea whose time had come by 1980. But in reality the federal budget position was better in 1980 than it had been at the time of the 1976 reauthorization, with the deficit down from 24.7 percent of revenues to 14.3 percent.[48] Federal individual income tax collections had just grown 20 percent in 1979.[49] While near-hysteria over the deficit was on the rise, there were other politics at work.

There were in particular two spending areas seen as being prime claimants to any revenue growth—a social security system coming under scrutiny for projected shortfalls and a perceived need to reverse the decline in defense spending. The former had millions of senior citizens lobbying for it, and the latter had a defense industry suddenly backed by a U.S. citizenry held hostage along with the captives in Iran. Governors, whose endorsements no longer mattered much in elections driven by media buys and the campaign contributions necessary to fund them, didn't have much of a chance. The political arena, and the relative power of its participants, was undergoing an important change.

THE 1983 REAUTHORIZATION:
LOCAL GOVERNMENTS HANG ON

The state–local lobby coalition had clearly been showing signs of weakness. Of the $35.1 billion in budget cuts approved by Congress in 1981, more than one-third, about $13 billion, came out of federal grants.[50]

It had been taken as a bad sign that while in 1980 President Carter and the Senate had wanted to extend the revenue sharing program for five years for local governments, the ultimately approved bill specified only three. Setting what would become the lowered expectations tone for the 1983 reauthorization, Senator Durenberger (R-MN) said, "If all we can accomplish this year is a simple reauthorization, let's be satisfied with that."[51] It was all they could accomplish.

There were, of course, several other possibilities, including a reduction in or termination of the program for local governments; formula changes to better target the funds to needier places; more funds for local governments; and the reinstatement of funds for state governments. President Reagan showed his ambivalence toward revenue sharing by including it in a revised Community Development Block Grant proposal, while at the same time providing in his budget for its extension at the existing $4.6 billion level for local governments, but for only one year.

By 1983 criticism of revenue sharing had become one-dimensional—the rising deficit meant that there was no revenue to share. President Reagan made sure of this. In pushing a program of supply-side economics, which relied on tax reductions and a huge build-up of defense spending, Reagan's initiatives ate up all of the room for expansion in other program areas. Federal expenditures for fiscal year 1983 were an astonishing 34.6 percent higher than revenues, a product of the recession, the tax cuts, and the defense build-up. The new federal budget era had truly arrived, an era in which there would be a shrinking pot of funds to vie for, with any gain won at the cost of some other program—dedistributive policy making.[52]

States rejoined the revenue sharing fray. They no longer had to defend surpluses—the National Conference of State Legislatures reported that at least thirty states would end their fiscal year in debt. Lobbyist Martin said at the time, "The fiscal condition of states is worse than it's ever been."[53] The state and local coalition re-formed to support renewed state participation in the program. Lobby groups of local governments were not entirely altruistic; as one lobbyist for the U.S. Conference of Mayors put it, "aid to states would forestall the states' own cuts in aid to cities."[54]

The lobbying seemed at first to work. The House Committee on Government Operations added the $2.3 billion for States to the program, but while they did away with the "dollar for dollar" swap with categoricals, they retained the requirement that the grants be appropriated, dimming its prospects. The full House, however, voted by the slim margin of 218–193 to eliminate the authorization for states. The closeness of the vote might seem surprising. There were probably not this many true supporters of the state share; knowing that the authorization would likely be denied by the Appropriations Committee made a "yes" vote a "win–win" situation, allowing members of Congress to be able to seem responsive to their states without adding to the deficit. The sponsor of the amendment to remove the states, Rep. Al McCandless (R-CA), admitted as much:

> Frankly, I see no reason to continue the charade. Revenue sharing funds for the states have not been appropriated since 1980, and I honestly doubt that our budget will allow appropriation in the next three years. Let us be honest with the governors and state legislators and tell them there will be no state share by entitlement or through the appropriations process.[55]

Ironically, there was no serious attempt to add the States in the Senate, the chamber of Congress which more directly represents them.

Local governments would fare better. There were several factors working in their favor. As they were still in the program, continuing their participation would not involve additional deficit spending. From a need point of view, the fiscal squeeze that many local governments faced, particularly central cities, had not eased and had been exacerbated by the recession. Moreover, one of the great and growing social ills of the 1980s had found a name and was gaining attention at all levels of government. Homelessness was an embarrassing phenomenon for a country that prided itself on being the greatest nation on earth. The increasing impact of the "Tax Revolt" also made it difficult for local governments in particular to respond to basic needs.

The House Government Operations Committee voted to reauthorize revenue sharing for local governments for five years, with a slight increase in funding from $4.7 billion to $5.3 billion, rejecting the revised Reagan request for a three-year renewal at current levels. It was argued that the extra funding was to make up for inflationary erosion in local allocations. There were also formula issues debated, including a defeated proposal by Rep. Lyle Williams (R-OH) to allocate $350 million of the annual increase in revenue sharing to counties with an unemployment rate of 15 percent or more. Several other attempts to change the funding formula were also defeated. In addition, Congressman Weiss had initially intended to offer a $1.25 billion counter-cyclical aid package to state and local governments, but withheld it because he did not want to endanger revenue sharing.

The Senate Finance Committee voted unanimously to reauthorize the program for three years at current funding levels, accepting the Reagan proposal. The committee added an unusual provision, however. If the House added more funding, the formula for distribution would be changed. The formula change was championed by Senator Durenberger and was meant to correct for what was seen as a distortion in allocation due to the use of taxes per capita as a measure of tax effort. This overestimated the burden for states like Alaska and Texas, which exported much of their state tax burden through taxes on oil, ultimately paid by consumers across the nation. Providing more evidence of how difficult it is to change formulas, the adopted proposal would have given certain local governments an increase by removing inequities in the current formula, but also would hold harmless every local government, so that none would get less than they otherwise would have.

A letter from Treasury Secretary Regan to Senator John Heinz (R-PA) had raised the hopes of those pushing for the formula change and extra funding. It said that while the administration "would specifically find objectionable" an increase in funding under the existing formula because it was "flawed," a funding increase under the Durenberger changes "would be considerably less objectionable."[56]

The committee proposal was unusual in that it would be triggered by House action. Even more unusual was the process by which it was passed. Chairman Robert Dole (R-KS) let absent committee members vote on the formula change after the bill had been reported by committee. This is usually allowed only if the votes do not change the outcome. In this case, the absent votes helped turn what had been an 8–10 loss in markup to a 10–8 victory—a lot of intrigue for a provision that was fairly moderate and destined to be unsuccessful. The committee did explicitly reject by 5–11 a proposal by Senator Daniel Patrick Moynihan (D-NY) to add an inflation-adjusting $450 million per year to the program.

The full House approved reauthorization of revenue sharing for three years, as opposed to the five requested by committee, by a close vote of 226–202, and with a vote of 381–35 raised funding from the existing $4.6 billion to $5.02 billion, less than what their committee recommended but within the congressional budget resolution. Budget director David Stockman said this was still $450 million a year too much. The House also rejected every attempt to change the formula, including one targeted at localities with high unemployment and another seeking to substitute a more accurate measure of tax effort, which had been developed by the ACIR and championed in the Senate by Durenberger, for the existing measure. The latter amendment failed by 192–220, a surprisingly close margin for a rather technical change, although it would have resulted in helping local governments in states where there was real tax strain. The final bill passed 381–43, again a remarkable show of support in tight fiscal times.

The Senate stayed with the recommendations of its committee and voted 87–6 to reauthorize for three years at existing funding levels. During debate the "trigger" provision of the Finance Committee was dropped by voice vote at the request of Sen. Russell Long (D-LA), who noted that the House had already reduced their increase in the program. But he also warned of the implications of changing the formula. He said such a move would be difficult to justify to jurisdictions that did not get an increase and, summing up the difficulty of changing formulas, said it "would be a lot better for every senator" not to have to explain anything.[57] The Senate also explicitly rejected an increase in funds for the program by a vote of 30–64.

On November 17 Congress approved a three-year extension of federal revenue sharing at existing levels. This time it was the Senate that played hardball, telling House conferees they could "take it or leave it." House conferee Ted Weiss complained about the lack of negotiation over raising the funding level, but all of the Senate conferees were members of the Finance Committee, deeply concerned with the budget deficit. State authorization was removed, and several other minor provisions were approved. In a further sign of the not-too-happy times, one provided that a local government whose tax base fell by 20 percent or more due to a plant closing or other economic hardship would be protected from any reduction in revenue sharing funds. In recognizing that the public participation requirements had little effect, the law also eliminated the requirement that there be a local hearing on possible uses of the funds before a hearing on proposed uses. Finally, it also called on the Secretary of the Treasury to conduct a study of the program, particularly its formula.

It was reported that the Senate approved revenue sharing "in a mild-mannered debate lasting a mere two hours...."[58] "Mild-mannered" best sums up the 1983 reauthorization debate overall—there was little excitement. Indeed, some of the most prolonged discussion came over the measurement of tax effort in the distribution formula. Thus debate over revenue sharing had come from disagreements between those opposed to a sacrilegious loss of congressional control over funds and those expecting a burst of creative energy to the technical point of measuring tax effort. The bolder ideas, such as one by Senator Durenberger to set up a permanent revenue sharing trust fund of 4 percent of federal individual income tax collections and offset the cost by limiting the deductibility of state and local taxes, were never really considered.

The fragility of the revenue sharing coalition was reaffirmed with each attempt to change the distribution formula. When faced with the new Senate formula which would be triggered by an increase in the revenue sharing allocation, the House backed down, fearful of Rep. Frank Horton's (R-NY) warning that ". . . altering the formula could, quite simply, endanger the fragile coalition that supports the program and spell its demise."[59] Earlier the House had rejected a similar amendment by Rep. Carl Levin, even though he tempered it with a 10 percent cap on how much of an increase a deserving locality could get. Congressman Bill Richardson (D-NM) reminded his colleagues that the change to the ACIR index of tax capacity and effort would reduce funding for eleven of thirteen Western states, and Rep. Weiss said "he feared the change would disrupt the political coalition that supports revenue sharing."[60]

It was becoming clear that the federal deficit was not going to go away, that it would remain the dominant policy issue for many years.

Along with the performance of the economy, this made the environment in which revenue sharing was renewed an unhappy one, full of difficult choices. The recession certainly gave an added importance to renewal of the local share. Senator Heinz said:

> At this time, in the midst of a recession would be the worst possible time to end general revenue sharing. It is the local safety net that succeeds, where the federal safety net doesn't.[61]

One has to wonder whether revenue sharing would have survived if there hadn't been a recession at the time. One would not have to wonder for long.

1985–1986: THE DEATH OF GENERAL REVENUE SHARING

General Revenue Sharing was formally scheduled to expire on September 30, 1986, unless reauthorized. "New Federalist" President Ronald Reagan took away any drama by proposing its elimination in a February 21, 1985, press conference:

> It doesn't make sense for a federal government running a deficit to be borrowing money to be spent by state and local governments that are now running surpluses.[62]

The president, who in 1981 had told a state–local coalition that "he had no intention of balancing the budget on the backs of state and local governments," was doing an about-face.[63]

In an era of deficit reduction frenzy, the termination of revenue sharing would cut federal spending by $3.5 billion in fiscal 1987, and $4.9 billion in fiscal 1988. An important report by the Treasury Department had implied that state and local governments could handle the loss.[64] By the spring, the *Congressional Quarterly Weekly Report* noted that "General Revenue Sharing has achieved the dubious honor of being the only federal program slated for elimination in both the House and Senate budget resolutions."[65] It had come a long way from the overwhelming show of support it had experienced in floor votes as recently as 1983.

The argument that a federal government in deficit could no longer afford to share revenue with local units of government, a growing criticism over the life of the program, had finally matured. As a percentage of revenues, deficits had stubbornly stayed near 28 percent since the last reauthorization of revenue sharing in 1983. Along with tax reform, deficit reduction had become the most important priority of

Congress and the President, culminating in the passage of the Gramm–Rudman–Hollings bill, which called for automatic across-the-board expenditure cuts if deficit targets were not met.[66] There was no longer any criticism of the revenue sharing program or its merits; it had just become a question of whether or not the federal government could afford it.

Local officials argued vehemently for continuation, with some of the strongest rhetoric coming from rural counties and small communities where revenue sharing made up a large portion of the local budget, and where it could be argued that revenue sharing should not have been sent in the first place. State and local governments, flush with revenues from tax increases they were forced to impose during the previous recession, had sizeable surpluses in the aggregate—5.5 percent and 6.1 percent, respectively—making it difficult to plead poverty.

Still, it was argued that terminating the program would force local property tax increases and expenditure cuts. Members of Congress were reminded that local revenue-raising powers were limited legally, making response even more difficult. Most importantly, they noted, there should be no cut in the allocation for the final year, as local governments had already included it in their budgets.

There were bills introduced in both houses of Congress in 1985 and 1986 to extend revenue sharing beyond 1986, some for three years, some for five, one for seven, some subjecting the program to annual appropriations, some not. There was also a proposal floated to give local governments the option, as states had, of trading categorical dollars for revenue sharing funds. But this was all for naught—revenue sharing was going down. In fact, it took a great deal of effort to prevent a reduction in the final year's allocation; Reagan not only confirmed his intention to terminate the program by not including it in his fiscal 1987 budget proposal, but had proposed rescinding $760 million of it in fiscal 1986.

The only floor vote was in the Senate, which rejected by 54–41 Senator Moynihan's (D-NY) amendment to fund the program for another year, with provision of equivalent revenues, a requirement of the fiscal year 1987 congressional budget resolution. The House Government Operations Committee voted to approve the program for three years, but it was never taken up by the full House. Meanwhile, the director of the Office of Revenue Sharing was requesting $5.6 million in fiscal 1987 to close down his office.

So General Revenue Sharing died in undramatic fashion, victim of a congressional budget resolution, without even a full hearing on its merits on the House floor.[67] There were many potential targets of deficit cutters; why was General Revenue Sharing cut? After all, as Rep. Roman

Mazzoli of New York had argued, ". . . because funding for GRS has been frozen at the same $4.6 billion figure since 1980, it is not a villain in the federal deficit drama."[68]

It was cut because it was an easy target. First, it was a large and concentrated number. As Congressman Robert Walker (R-PA) pointed out, it "was $5 billion in money in one pot that could be dealt with in one fell swoop. It made a tempting target."[69] Second, the fact that state and local governments were seen as being in good financial condition that year made it easier to pull the trigger. This was expedient, but odd reasoning. The Michigan state treasurer, Robert Bowman, offered:

> There appears to be a philosophy that state and local governments, because they dealt with the '82 and '83 crises by raising taxes and cutting spending, because we had the wherewithal to handle the budget crisis, that therefore we ought to be punished.[70]

Indeed, many state and local officials did feel that they were being punished for doing the right thing fiscally, while their federal counterparts irresponsibly cut taxes and ran up spending in other areas, producing the deficits that had all of Washington's attention. Congress had the power to raise taxes, too. The termination of revenue sharing was characterized by a lobbyist for the National League of Cities as "Let's pass the buck to state and local officials. Let them make the difficult decisions."[71] And there were some who thought the panic over the deficit was out of proportion to its importance in the first place. Budget expert Aaron Wildavsky pointed out that many of the predicted negative economic consequences of large deficits were not occurring, and said it is "a difficulty, I contend, but it is not a disaster next to which all else is insignificant."[72]

The third reason why General Revenue Sharing was one of the most significant trophies in the 1985–1986 deficit-reduction hunt had to do with the nature of its benefits and beneficiaries. Because the funds could be used in any way local officials desired, it blended with other local revenues and therefore usually was not the entire source of support for any specific activity. This allowed Congress to avoid taking responsibility for specific cuts. The local discretion and responsibility which had antagonized many members of Congress became an asset in deficit reduction.

Then there were the governmental beneficiaries themselves, who suffered from the diversity of their members. Any attempt to reform revenue sharing, and thus potentially make it more justifiable, met with opposition. After "more money" and "more discretion," state and local officials often find it hard to agree. Had the program's formula been changed to make it more redistributive, it might have had a better chance of survival.

Further, all (political) power being relative, state and local elected officials were at a disadvantage compared to other claimants in the fight to protect their programs. Diffuse benefits produce few vocal supporters for a program like revenue sharing, which had to compete for resources in the new deficit-reduction world. And other, more narrowly targeted, interest groups have the advantage of being able to donate large sums of money to congressional campaigns. As John Petersen of the Government Finance Officers of America pointed out at the time: "Public interest groups don't deal in the currency that sways the hearts and minds of Congress—namely political action committees."[73] Well before the mid-1980s congressional campaigns were being won with elaborate media campaigns financed by campaign contributions, not by endorsements from state and local elected officials. Nor are the public interest lobbyists well bankrolled. As the National League of Cities' Frank Shafroth admitted, "We can't compete against the home builders and the Realtors."[74]

No wonder, then, that Charles McLure, Jr., a deputy assistant secretary of the treasury in 1985, told an advisory panel of representatives of state and local governments, "We talk sometimes as though we're in different countries."[75] There certainly were very different political dynamics at work.

After distributing over $83 billion in fourteen years to 39,000 localities, revenue sharing was no more. To a great extent it ended, like T.S. Eliot's world, not with a bang but a whimper.

ANALYSIS

There are very few programs of the magnitude of General Revenue Sharing of which it can be said that it was remarkable that it was enacted at all and remarkable that it was ended. But such is the unique history of the federal revenue sharing. At its passage, the policy arguments both for and against it were for the most part valid. So what tipped the scales? The timing was right. In 1972 the federal government was in relatively sound fiscal shape, there was growing criticism of the existing federal grant system, and state and local officials lobbied hard at a time when their campaign support still meant a lot electorally. Its defeat was due to several factors, including perhaps how local governments had used the funds and confusion over the program's purpose, but timing was also important in 1986; reducing the federal budget deficit was paramount, the state–local coalition had weakened, and there was an intellectual shift toward public choice theory and "competitive federalism."

Local Impact

Was the General Revenue Sharing program a success or a failure? This is a difficult question to answer, and when that is true a program's fate will be greatly influenced by other factors. Differing versions of a program's goals can help in its passage, but this makes evaluation difficult and renewal problematic. Revenue sharing certainly was administratively efficient, but that should have been expected of a program that just mailed checks from Washington to 39,000 units of local government. Still, by doing so revenue sharing provided mild fiscal relief to recipient governments, and thus reduced the overall regressivity of the U.S. federal fiscal system a little. But much more had been expected.

Proponents of revenue sharing, in hyperbole most likely deemed necessary to sell the program, had promised a dramatic impact, with creative uses springing from reinvigorated local decision making. This should not have been expected to happen, and it didn't. Local officials, constrained by balanced budget requirements and fearful of beginning programs they would have to fund from local sources should revenue sharing end, disproportionately spent early allocations for capital improvement purposes, which would provide the maximum benefit now with low cost later. At the local level, as opposed to the federal, what was fiscally right was also politically right—being cautious. The importance of uncertainty over the new form of federal aid was readily admitted, and, of course, local officials were ultimately proven correct—revenue sharing was ended. There was uncertainty over other federal programs, too, but under those grants local officials did not have the freedom of use which revenue sharing allowed. Cuts in programs without local discretion could be blamed on Washington.

As time wore on and the relative size of revenue sharing funds in local budgets shrank, local officials came to treat the funds like any other general revenues and used them to fund the services they were already providing. It is important to note that this use, to support existing programs and in effect substitute for local revenue, was not by itself fatal to the program. In fact, the 1976 reauthorization even took out the priority use requirement and prohibition on use of revenue sharing funds to match other federal funds, in effect at least statutorily condoning any use by local officials. Political ramifications proved different.

Nor were the uses for capital improvements or to maintain existing services indefensible. In the former case, revenue sharing allowed cities to undertake projects that they most likely had been unable to fund and reduced borrowing costs. The use to maintain existing services allowed cities to avoid cutbacks in basic services at a time of rapidly increasing costs and lessened the burden on the property tax, a regressive source of revenue. While other federal and state programs may have been pursuing worthy goals, their success is always partly dependent on the basic city service structure, which revenue sharing was supporting.

But for many the fact that there was no dramatic impact of the program meant that it could only be defended for its ability to correct for vertical fiscal imbalance, the greater ability of the federal government to raise revenue and the advantage of state and local governments in determining needs and providing services, and/or to compensate for horizontal fiscal imbalance, the differing fiscal capacities and needs of states and local governments, the "rich government, poor government" problem of the subnational level.[76]

The inability of Congress to gain enough support to change the formula for allocation of revenue sharing funds to make it more redistributive made it difficult to defend the program on these grounds. While mildly redistributive, it became clear that there was not enough consensus to make revenue sharing truly so. As for vertical fiscal imbalance, it could (and can) still be argued in theory that it is easier for the federal government to raise revenue than it is for state and local governments, but in practice this has not been the case. For federal officials, as opposed to local officials, good electoral politics in the 1980s meant doing what was fiscally irresponsible—granting large tax cuts and increasing program benefits, ultimately producing troublesome deficits. Federal elected officials resisted taking advantage of their superior revenue-raising ability.

The Deficit

When opponents of revenue sharing such as Congressman Brooks said "We've got no revenue to share," they were, of course, not speaking the entire truth. Congress was sharing its revenue (and borrowed money) with plenty of beneficiaries through many programs; revenue sharing was just ultimately not to be one of them. As was pointed out in Chapter Two, there were judicial, political, and fiscal reasons for the rise of the federal government's role in the federal system; the latter two would once again alter its character.

The need to reduce the federal budget deficit was the policy rationale used to kill revenue sharing. Ironically, while its critics had rallied against its separation of taxing and spending, the most important separation of taxing and spending was occurring annually in the federal budget. Revenue sharing was enacted in response to problems created by Washington policy makers—the increasingly burdensome and regulated nature of the federal grant system—and it would be terminated to a great extent as a result of other sins of Congress.

State and local governments could argue that they had little to do with the run-up of federal budget deficits in the 1980s. In fact, federal grants fell as a percentage of state–local outlays from 25.8 percent in 1980 to 17.3 percent in 1989.[77] The drop in aid to city governments was even more dramatic. What did produce the increase in the deficit? Indexation of the federal individual income tax for inflation slowed revenue growth. Other causes included the slowdown in real annual per capita economic growth from the unusually high 2.24 percent from 1948 to 1973 to the more historically based 1.4 percent from 1973 through 1995; the growth in the cost of entitlement programs, particularly Medicare and Medicaid, due to increased eligibility, expanded services, and inflation in the health care sector; the double-digit inflation of the 1970s followed by recession; and in the 1980s, President Reagan's twin policies of tax cuts and a defense build-up.[78] The latter action was seen by some as a conspiracy aimed at making the deficit so large that the size of government (and particularly social programs) would be reduced, a charge similar to that made of President Nixon's attempt to use a budget gap to cut back funds for Great Society programs.[79]

The argument was made, both in 1980 in terminating States, and in 1986 when the local share of revenue sharing ended, that these subnational units of government were in better fiscal shape than Washington and therefore shouldn't receive the funds. By being fiscally responsible, state and local governments drew the budget-cutting wrath of Congress. This was selective reasoning on the part of Washington, as having one's books in balance at the end of a fiscal year is not necessarily a sign of fiscal ability, but political will. Members of Congress, like their state and local counterparts, could have raised taxes to solve their fiscal problem. And while the timing was good in those particular years in that state and then local balances were high, they would show their proposensity to cycle lower in each case in the years following.

As Congressman Wyler pointed out, the rationale of state–local balance/federal imbalance could be used to argue for cutting any and all federal aid. Why revenue sharing? There were several things that made it an easy deficit reduction target, as already noted. At $4.2 billion, the local share was a nice target, all in one line item. Its benefits were diffuse, and therefore Congress would not suffer the wrath of organized local interests angry at program cuts. Even if there were objections from local groups, Congress could blame state and local officials, saying that they could pick up funding for any scaled-back service. Thus, cutting revenue sharing was a natural, giving Congress deficit savings with little pain. They felt they had never received much political credit from the program in the first place. In the 1988 survey in this study, local officials were asked why they felt that Washington favored categorical grants over revenue sharing, and the leading response at 46 percent was "political credit" (Table 4-1).

There were certainly other programs that survived with weaker rationales. The National Wool Act, for example, was left over from the Korean War, when wool shortages threatened the production of uniforms. Since early 1960 the uniforms have been made of synthetic material, yet the subsidy continued. Or the huge subsidies for tobacco growers, when the nation is trying to discourage smoking. The subsidy to the Tennessee Valley Authority was questionable. There was more to the ease with which Congress cut General Revenue Sharing.

The State and Local Lobby

How could a program which benefited 39,000 units of local government not have a powerful lobby? Because, as one former member of the Treasury Department put it, "support for revenue sharing was a mile wide and an inch deep."[80] The nature of revenue sharing made it more difficult for the lobby to be as successful as it could be with other federal grants.

The second leading response to the question, "why does Washington seemingly favor categorical grants over revenue sharing," at 19 percent, was interest group backing (Table 4-1). This accurately reflects the fact that it is easier to muster support from several arenas for a categorical grant program than it is for a program of unrestricted aid. Local beneficiaries of a grant program, both suppliers and recipients, often allied with a national interest group, will join local elected officials

---

TABLE 4-1
Why Does Washington Favor Categorical Grants?

	No.	%
Political Credit	37	46%
Interest Group Backing	15	19
More Control/Accountability	12	15
Ability to Target	12	15
Bureaucratic Support	2	2
Other	3	4
	$N = 81$	

in fighting against a proposed cut in a federal categorical aid program. The federal bureaucracy administering the program will join the fray, as might members of the relevant substantive congressional committee or subcommittee, fleshing out the classic iron triangle. Revenue sharing did not have this range of support, in a way similar to Nixon's guaranteed annual income proposal, also doomed to failure.[81]

As the purchasing power of the fixed revenue sharing grant fell over time, there was less incentive to lobby hard for its continuance. The fact that fiscal times were good for both states and local governments when they were cut also may have made them a little lazy. Further, being a mile wide and an inch deep—that is, spreading revenue sharing funds over all units of local government, needy or not—reduced the amount that each got. Had those in need gotten more, the intensity of the lobbying effort of those governments would likely have been greater.

This need to include all, a fatal flaw of any interest group with great diversity, also gave opponents easy targets for criticism—why were federal tax dollars going to a place like Beverly Hills or Palm Springs? The inability to reform the program's formula to make it more redistributive took away a potential line of defense. Conflict over change neutralized the state–local lobby, paralyzing them in the debate over formula change. This made them defenders of the status quo, even when the status quo was becoming increasingly indefensible. For categorical grant programs, congressional legislation usually sets out the broad guidelines for the program, and it is administered by a federal bureaucracy, which makes many important distributional decisions. With revenue sharing, the guidelines *were* the distribution, highlighting the importance of any proposed changes and making them an easy target of political pressure. A National League of Cities official admitted, "Targeting hurts our big dues payers."[82]

The inability of state–local interest groups to agree to target is of course reenforced by the structure of Congress, where each member feels compelled to make sure that in any program his or her district or state does as well as any other. This always makes intergovernmental policy making difficult in a federal system, but more so when the benefits are explicitly designated in the law, and so clearly measurable. In a classic Catch-22 situation, the federal government, according to all theories of fiscal federalism, should be the level of government to undertake redistributive policy, yet congressional organization and electoral incentives make it difficult for it to overcome provinciality.[83] More targeting results in less support. This universal tendency has been reenforced by the fact that votes had long since moved from the areas of most need. Proposals to alter the revenue sharing distribution formula were made by both presidents and members of Congress, but never came close to passage. The fact that money was going to places without need made it easier to justify ending the program.

Then there is the problem of the state–local lobby competing in the larger budgetary arena. It may have some success when dealing with an all-federal-aid issue, such as mandate relief, but when it is competing with other organized interest groups for limited federal resources it is at a distinct disadvantage.

The Kennedy–Nixon debates of 1960 highlighted the importance of television and forever changed the face of campaigns for national offices in America. Media expenses dominate campaign spending. The influence of special interest money is hotly debated, with some arguing that since it is not illegal, there is nothing wrong with it. Members of Congress who look out for campaign contributors are merely doing constituent service.

While state and local officials can offer endorsements and appear at fund-raisers, other interest groups, through political action committees, can raise the funds which candidates desperately need to compete. It would follow that these groups are more likely to get the ear of a member of Congress, and have a chance at protecting their targeted interest, than are public interest groups who are unable to contribute funds and for whom it can always be argued that they have their own tax-raising powers to fund programs. In fact, at a meeting of state legislators and Senator Muskie in 1979, Muskie exploded over their support of a balanced budget amendment to the constitution, threatening, "I can balance the federal budget tomorrow by cutting all aid to state and local governments, and let you raise the funds yourselves."[84]

Former Congressman Abner Mikva (D-IL) admitted that members of Congress have "little or no loyalty to the state organization" when they take office.[85] Huckshorn and Bibby have elaborated:

> Congressional and Senatorial candidates must rely heavily on nonparty sources for funds. Therefore, representatives and senators, once in office, feel little sense of obligation to their state and local parties, and the parties lack significant influence on the behavior of legislators in the halls of Congress.[86]

If spending cuts are necessary to try to balance the federal budget, members of Congress are more likely then to protect programs favoring realtors or bankers than they are state and local elected officials, or to protect Medicare and Social Security, with the most powerful lobby in Washington, DC—the American Association of Retired Persons (AARP)—than to renew a program like revenue sharing. When asked in separate interviews why federal aid other than Medicaid had fallen, ACIR's John Shannon and the National Governors Association's Jim Martin both replied with a single acronym—"AARP." Any health care program can muster support from beneficiaries and providers, including hospitals, doctors, and insurance and medical supply companies— and each of their professional associations. State and local officials can't compete.

In fact, it was during the debate over the deficit cutting of 1985 and 1986 and revenue sharing's place in it that state and local government representatives first explicitly admitted this inferiority in the national political arena—that they couldn't compete with the homebuilders and the realtors. While political might does not always make right, it does protect some programs at the expense of others.

The Politics of Ideas

John Kingdon has written that it is essential for those interested in explaining public policy to look at the importance of ideas, and how they are developed, in addition to looking at political power and pressure.[87] Beam, Conlan, and Wrightson nicely elaborate on the importance of ideas in explaining passage of the 1986 tax reform.[88] Similarly, while an autopsy of General Revenue Sharing will find politics and deficit reduction as the primary cause of death, it will also find revenue sharing to have been swimming against the intellectual tide of the mid-1980s.

In an odd way, revenue sharing, born to give more power to the states, fell victim to the rising ideology that more responsibility should be given to the states. President Nixon started the anti-Washington rhetoric with his calls for a New Federalism in 1971, and every successful presidential candidate since, except George Bush, had most recently been a governor and used their "outsider" status prominently in their campaigns. But it was Ronald Reagan who really turned the tide against the federal government.

Reagan tapped into the rising feeling that government had gotten too big and too removed from the citizenry, and fueled its flames. Besides his rhetoric,

> . . . Reagan's series of initiatives (the 1981 tax cut, the block grants, the proposed swap of program responsibilities, 1986 tax reform, and the constant pressure on domestic spending) accelerated the swing of the pendulum away from federal power towards increased state responsibility.[89]

The simple solution, then, was letting government decisions be made closer to the people.

There was also at this time a tremendous resurgence among academics in interest in public or rational choice theory, promoting the benefits of competition among governments, and this filtered its way into the policy world. Daniel Schwallie commented:

> Perhaps the recent developments in intergovernmental grant theory reflect an ideological shift within the economics professions toward decentralized fiscal federalism. Perhaps they reflect a post-Watergate cynicism toward government. Or perhaps they merely reflect a realization, born out of experience, that there are practical limits to what can be accomplished with grants-in-aid and that these limits need definition.[90]

Charles Tiebout's model of "voting with your feet," which had been applied more fully to federalism by Wallace Oates, was appealing in its simple argument that governments would become more efficient if they truly had to compete for taxpayers.[91]

A program of unrestricted aid like revenue sharing, then, was seen as distorting the federalism "market." If states and local governments were truly to compete, they should do so free of any financial bias introduced by Washington. This is ironic, in that revenue sharing was seen as the federal aid program that least distorted local decisions. Nevertheless, the feeling was that forcing state and local governments to raise their own revenue would make them more efficient, and revenue sharing interfered with that dynamic.

The public choice model has many flaws, of course, not the least being the fact that it, like any market model, assumes perfect information and mobility. This favors higher income taxpayers, who may indeed seek out efficient tax havens, leaving the poor to fend for themselves. Equity is not a concern of public choice theory. The use of a market model must also include the possibility that some competitors will go out of business. This can't be allowed for governments. Nevertheless, this paradigm has provided the basis for the continuing move toward devolution/decentralization.

At its passage in 1972, revenue sharing had to fight off the criticism that it didn't fit with the prevailing wisdom on structure of local governments; it was accused of propping up inefficient ones and thus slowing the movement toward consolidation and regionalism. Large governments were good. In the mid-1980s revenue sharing was once more found to be propping up governments, but this time interfering with the dominant notion that governments should compete by their own means, that more governments are better than fewer. The first time it had enough political support to overcome the criticism; the second time it didn't.

In 1980 Leonard Robins argued in "The Plot that Succeeded" that Richard Nixon's New Federalism should not have been judged by the specific policy initiatives he offered, most of which failed, but by its weakening of the legitimacy of the Washington establishment and creation of the neoconservative movement.[92] In viewing federal intergovernmental policy of the 1980s and early 1990s, it would appear that the reality finally caught up with the earlier rhetoric.

SUMMARY

There was a not-so-surprising parallel between the life of General Revenue Sharing at the city and federal levels. As the program went from being an exciting infusion of new funds in a new form at the local level to just another source of revenue, so would it go in Washington from being a much heralded reform of the federal grant system and federalism itself to just another program which could be sacrificed to deficit reduction. At both levels, it went from the very interesting to the rather mundane.

General Revenue Sharing would seem to be an idea whose time came and went, at least politically. Given the importance of the politics of ideas, it might have done better if it had been named "federal income tax sharing" or "the fiscal equalization grant." Maybe it would have gotten more respect; at least it would have made it more difficult for opponents to use the too easily understood slogan, "We've got no revenue to share."

The history of revenue sharing also shows the difficulty of formulating sound intergovernmental policy and the greater difficulty of reforming it once it's in place. Communication between the federal officials and their state and local counterparts was clearly selective at the time of passage, if one judges by the expectations for the program announced in Washington. The many conflicting views as to the hoped-for impact of revenue sharing, while helping passage, also made it difficult to evaluate and thus to justify. There was some discussion of reformulating it to send more money to poor places, but any move to make it more redistributive was unacceptable as it inherently produced less support in Congress. And again, while a more redistributive program might have been easier to defend, it would have had more difficulty gaining passage in the first place.

Nor were the public interest groups representing state and local governments able to agree on any formula changes, even if it would have taken away the criticism that the program was wasteful in that it sent money to places that didn't need it. This left the program to be justified on the basis of providing mild fiscal relief and putting a small dent in the overall regressivity of the state–local tax system, not enough to defend itself against the steamroller issue of the day, federal deficit reduction.

In a scenario with some irony, state and local officials got themselves in trouble by doing the right thing fiscally, and balancing their budgets, often by raising taxes. Meanwhile the federal government not only refused to show the same fiscal responsibility, but used the fiscal position of state and local governments as an argument for terminating revenue sharing.

The state–local lobby was very powerful at the time of passage of General Revenue Sharing, yet unable to protect it in the 1980s, even though it had become a much smaller part of the federal government budget. The importance of the drive to reduce the budget deficit in the death of revenue sharing cannot be denied, but other, less worthy programs survived, proving the relative weakness of state and local officials.

Ronald Reagan finished what Richard Nixon started, in both the narrow and broad sense. In killing General Revenue Sharing, Reagan finished off what had been the cornerstone of Nixon's New Federalism. But more broadly, this action and others also brought the anti-Washington, pro-State direction of domestic policy to fruition, for better or for worse, a trend carried on by President Clinton and the Republican Congress.

Some of the arguments used to pass revenue sharing, such as the plight of needy local governments, are still valid today. Had the program been reformed to make it more targeted to places of need, it might have survived. But in an odd sense it has survived, the subject of the next chapter.

NOTES

1. Office of the Federal Register National Archives and Records Administration, "Remarks on Signing the Local Government Fiscal Assistance Amendments of 1983," Public Papers of the President: Ronald Reagan 1983, vol. II, (Washington, DC: U.S. Government Printing Office, 1983), p. 1633.

2. "Cities Seek Federal Aid to Ease Money Woes," Congressional Quarterly Weekly, Reprint, September 27, 1975, p. 2053.

3. Much of this discussion comes from "Cities Seek. . ," pp. 2053–2059.

4. "Revenue Sharing Markup," Congressional Quarterly Weekly Report, March 20, 1976, p. 661.

5. "Revenue Sharing Markup," p. 2055.

6. "Cities Seek. . . ," p. 2058.

7. "Revenue Sharing Markup," Congressional Quarterly Weekly Report, March 20, 1976, p. 661.

8. "Cities Seek...," p. 2057.

9. Joel Havemann, "Is the Revenue Sharing Lobby Coming Unstrung?" *National Journal*, July 10, 1976, pp. 966–967.

10. "House Passes Revenue Sharing Extension," *Congressional Quarterly Weekly Report*, June 12, 1986, p. 1541

11. "House passes...," p. 1542.

12. "Senate Votes to Extend Revenue Sharing Program," *Congressional Quarterly Weekly*, Reprint, Sept. 18, 1976, p. 2512.

13. "Senate Votes to Extend...," p. 2512.

14. "Statement of Hon. Kenneth A. Gibson, Mayor of the City of Newark, N.J., in *General Revenue Sharing*, Hearings Before the Subcommittee on Revenue Sharing of the Committee on Finance, United States Senate, Ninety-fourth Congress, First Session (Washington, DC: U.S. Government Printing Office, 1975), p. 49.

15. "Senate Votes to Extend...," p. 2512.

16. "Senate Votes to Extend...," p. 2512.

17. See George D. Brown, "Beyond the New Federalism—Revenue Sharing in Perspective," *Harvard Journal on Legislation* 15, no.1 (1977):1–73.

18. Joel Havemann, "New Federalism Report—Revenue sharing plan likely to be extended, changed," *National Journal Reports*, July 20, 1974, pp. 1074–1082, at 1074.

19. See, for example, M. Gottdiener, *The Decline of Urban Politics* (Beverly Hills, CA: Sage, 1987).

20. "Ford to the Governors," *Congressional Quarterly Weekly Report*, March 6, 1976, p. 526.

21. "Carter Revenue Sharing Text," *Congressional Quarterly Weekly Report*, April 26, 1980, p. 1132.

22. See John Shannon and Bruce Wallin, "Fiscal Imbalance Within the Federal System: The Problem of Renewing Revenue Sharing," in *Cities Under Stress*, ed. Robert W. Burchell and David Listokin (New Brunswick, NJ: Rutgers University Press, 1981):541–575.

23. See Shannon and Wallin, "Fiscal Imbalance...."

24. See Shannon and Wallin, "Fiscal Imbalance..."

25. Interview, Washington, DC, October 15, 1996. Martin also claims he got some measure of revenge by leaking to the *New York Times* a proposed formula change that would have sent nearly $100 million of the $500 million to New York City.

26. "Should Present Payments to State Governments Be Eliminated from the Federal Revenue Sharing Program," *Congressional Digest*, June 7, 1980, p. 184.

27. "Should Present Payments...," p. 184.

28. Rochelle L. Stanfield, "Revenue Sharing Survived this Year, But 1980 May Be a Different Story," *National Journal* 11, no. 32 (1979), p. 1331.

29. "Should Present Payments...," p. 188.

30. Will Myers and John Shannon, "Revenue Sharing for States: An Endangered Species," *Intergovernmental Perspective* 5, no. 3 (1979):10–17, at 12.

31. "Should Present Payments...," p. 171.

32. "Should Present Payments...," p.171.

33. Should Present Payments. . . ," p. 177.

34. "Should Present Payments. . . ," p. 177.

35. "Should Present Payments. . . ," p. 183.

36. James M. Howell and George D. Brown, "The Revenue Sharing Gauntlet: Fiscal Federalism at the Crossroads," *National Civic Review* 68, November 1979, pp. 535–541, at pp. 536–7.

37. Washington Post, May 1, 1980.

38. Neal R. Peirce and Jerry Hagsrom, "The Cities, Not the States, May Bear the Brunt of Revenue Sharing Cutbacks," *The National Journal* 12, no. 16 (1980):636

39. "State Grants in Doubt As House Panel Begins Revenue Sharing Markup," *Congressional Quarterly Weekly Report*, July 5, 1980, p. 1904.

40. "Revenue Sharing Decision Awaits Lame-Duck Session," *Congressional Quarterly Weekly Report*, October 25, 1980, p. 3217.

41. "Revenue Sharing Decision Awaits. . . ," p. 3217.

42. "House Votes to Restore Revenue Sharing for States; Anti-Recession Aid Dropped," *Congressional Quarterly Weekly Report*, November 15, 1980, p. 3361.

43. Jim Martin interview, Washington, DC, October 15, 1996.

44. Calculated from U.S. Advisory Commission on Intergovernmental Relations, *Significant Features of Fiscal Federalism, Volume 2: 1994*, Tables 31 and 41, p. 64 and p. 76.

45. "Cutbacks in State Revenue Sharing Test Public Interest Group Coalition," *Congressional Quarterly Weekly Report*, April 12, 1980, p. 952.

46. Peirce and Hagstrom, "The Cities Not the States. . ."

47. Martin Tolchin, "Senators Restore $572 Million in Aid for States in 1980," *New York Times*, June 28, 1980, p. 1.

48. U.S. Advisory Commission on Intergovernmental Relations, *Significant Features of Fiscal Federalism, Vol 2, 1994* (Washington, DC: ACIR, 1994): 23.

49. U.S. Advisory Commission, *Significant Features*, p. 68.

50. Craig T. Ferris, "Reaganomics '81: Little Joy for States, Cities," *Bond Buyer*, December 21, 1981, p. 1.

51. "State Aid, Formula Change Among Issues to Be Debated in Revenue Sharing Renewal," *Congressional Quarterly Weekly Report*, April 2, 1983, p. 659.

52. See Paul Light, *Artful Work: The Politics of Social Security Reform* (New York: Random House, 1985), pp. 15–16.

53. "State Aid, Formula Change. . . ," p. 660.

54. "State Aid, Formula Change. . . ," p. 660.

55. "House Approves Revenue Sharing Extension," *Congressional Quarterly Weekly Report*, August 6, 1983, p. 1608.

56. "Finance Panel Votes Changes in Revenue Sharing Formula," *Congressional Quarterly Weekly Report*, July 2, 1983, p. 1360.

57. "Senate Reauthorizes Funding For General Revenue Sharing," *Congressional Quarterly Weekly Report*, September 24, 1983, p. 1970.

58. "Senate Reauthorizes. . . ," p. 1970.

59. "House Approves. . . ," 1607.

60. "House Approves. . . ," p. 1608.

61. "State Aid, Formula Change. . . ," p. 659.

62. "39,000 Local Officials Await Decision on Revenue Sharing," *Congressional Quarterly Weekly Report*, March 2, 1985, p. 393.

63. Craig T. Ferris, "States, Localities Agree to Speak 'With One Voice' On Budget Cuts," *The Bond Buyer*, December 17, 1981, p. 3.

64. U.S. Department of the Treasury, Office of State and Local Finance, "Federal–State–Local Fiscal Relations," a Report to the President and the Congress (Washington, DC: U.S. Government Printing Office, 1985).

65. "General Revenue Sharing Targeted," *Congressional Quarterly Weekly Report*, May 25, 1985, p. 975.

66. See Aaron Wildavsky, *The New Politics of the Budgetary Process*, 2nd ed. (New York: Harper Collins, 1992), pp. 253–257.

67. Leslie A. Wollack, "House Leadership Kills Revenue Sharing," *Nation's Cities Weekly* September 29, 1986, pp. 8–9.

68. *Congressional Record–House*, January 30, 1986, p. H202.

69. "General Revenue Sharing Targeted. . . ," p. 975.

70. "State and Local Officials Fear Federal Budget, Tax Changes," *Congressional Quarterly Weekly Report*, January 12, 1985, p. 71.

71. "State and Local Officials Fear. . . ," p. 71.

72. *The New Politics of the Budgetary Process*, p. 472.

73. "State and Local Officials Fear. . . ," p. 74.

74. "State and Local Officials Fear. . . ," p. 72.

75. "State and Local Officials Fear. . . ," p. 72.

76. See Albert Davis and Robert Lucke, "The Rich-State–Poor-State Problem in a Federal System," *National Tax Journal* 35, no. 3 (1982):337–362.

77. U.S. Advisory Commission on Intergovernmental Relations, *Significant Features of Fiscal Federalism, 1994*, vol. II (Washington, DC: ACIR, 1994), table 10, p. 30.

78. Robert D. Reischauer, "Reducing the Deficit: Past Efforts and Future Challenges," The Frank M. Engle Lecture, May 6, 1996 (Bryn Mawr, Pennsylvania: The American College, 1996), pp. 8–10.

79. On Nixon, see Haider, *When Governments Come. . .*, p. 39; on Reagan, see John M. Quigley and Danied L. Rubinfeld, "Budget Reform and the Theory of Fiscal Federalism," *American Economic Review* 76 (1986):132–137, at 132.

80. Interview, Washington, DC, October 15, 1997.

81. Daniel Patrick Moynihan, *The Politics of a Guaranteed Annual Income: The Nixon Administration and the Family Assistance Plan* (New York: Random House, 1973).

82. Interview, Washington, DC, October 15, 1997.

83. On the redistributive role of the federal government see, for example, Richard A. Musgrave, *The Theory of Public Finance* (New York: McGraw Hill, 1959), and Paul E. Peterson, *City Limits* (Chicago: University of Chicago Press, 1981).

84. The author's recollection.

85. Abner J. Mikva and Patti B. Sarris, *The American Congress: The First Branch* (New York, NY: Franklin Watts, 1983), p. 70.

86. Robert Huckshorn and John Bibby, "State Parties in an Era of Political Change," in *The Future of American Political Parties*, ed. Joel Fleishman (Englewood Cliffs, NJ: Prentice Hall, 1982), pp. 91–92. Cited in ACIR, *The*

Transformation in American Politics: Implications for Federalism (Washington, DC: ACIR, 1986).

87. John W. Kingdon, *Agendas, Alternatives, and Public Policies* (Boston: Little, Brown, 1984), pp. 131–132.

88. David R. Beam, Timothy J. Conlan, and Margaret T. Wrightson, "Solving the Riddle of Tax Reform: Party Competition and the Politics of Ideas," *Political Science Quarterly* 105, no. 2, Summer 1990, 193–217.

89. John Shannon and James Edwin Kee, "The Rise of Competitive Federalism," *Public Budgeting and Finance* 9, no. 4 (1989):5–20, at 13.

90. Daniel P. Schwallie, *The Impact of Intergovernmental Grants on the Aggregate Public Sector* (New York: Quorum Books, 1989), p. 133.

91. See Charles Tiebout, "A Pure Theory of Local Expenditures," *Journal of Political Economy*, October, 1956, pp. 416–24; and Wallace Oates, *Fiscal Federalism* (New York, NY: Harcourt, Brace, Jovanovich, 1972).

92. Leonard Robins, "The Plot That Succeeded: The New Federalism as Policy Realignment," *Presidential Studies Quarterly* Winter, 1989, pp. 99–106.

5

Life After Death

The General Revenue Sharing experience helped to change the dynamics of intergovernmental relations in the United States and set the stage for the devolution movement of the 1990s. While cities survived the cut in funds, the lessons revenue sharing provides for intergovernmental aid policy are as important as the fiscal effects of its termination. Its history yields strong evidence of the difficulties inherent in enacting sound intergovernmental aid policy, and in later evaluating it.

General Revenue Sharing also played a role, intended or not, in changing the politics and therefore policy of the federal aid system. Debate over its reauthorization and its ultimate defeat affected the nature and strength of the state–local lobby. While state and local officials have recorded some victories since General Revenue Sharing was terminated, their power was reduced by the experience. Since then they have suffered some defeats in Congress, and are sometimes involved in federal policy making affecting them and at other times left out.[1]

With and without their participation, federal aid policy has continued to evolve since the end of GRS. Devolution and "fend-for-yourself" federalism became the buzzwords of the 1990s. The most dramatic example is the 1995 reform of welfare. There is more to come.

Yet even in this environment, the argument can be made that there is a place in a well-designed federal system for unrestricted federal aid to state and local governments. Indeed, revenue sharing lives on, most notably at the state level where unrestricted aid to their local units of government remains a consistent component of fiscal federalism. And while federal lawmakers have resisted the most blatant efforts to bring revenue sharing back, they have enacted programs which are very similar. This chapter will explore these themes.

CITY RESPONSE TO THE LOSS OF GRS

City officials never claimed that the termination of revenue sharing would be disastrous, and it wasn't. On average, General Revenue Sharing funds accounted for a little less than 3 percent of local government budgets by fiscal year 1985. But in some cities it meant more: 7 percent in Boston and 6.3 percent in Chicago, for example.[2] In whole numbers the loss seems more meaningful: Memphis and Cleveland, for example, each had to make do with $12 million less in annual revenue.

The survey in this study asked city officials how they responded to the loss of General Revenue Sharing. As Table 5-1 shows, the leading first choice in California was a reduction in capital improvement projects, mentioned by thirty-six of the sixty-five cities responding, followed by reduced operating expenditures and increases in user fees, each indicated by twenty-nine cities. The drop in capital improvement expenditures was to be expected in California—they had consistently indicated that they had used revenue sharing funds for that purpose. When the funds were gone, this spending had to be reduced. Reducing operating expenditures and increasing user fees were also logical responses from local chief executives who had their property tax options greatly limited, both legally and politically, by Proposition 13. Operat-

TABLE 5-1
Response to Loss of General Revenue Sharing

California

Response	Mentioned	%	1st Choice	%
Reduced operating exp.	29	45%	11	19%
Reduced cap. imp.	36	55%	23	40%
Raised local taxes	5	8%	1	2%
Increased fees, licenses	29	45%	7	12%
Used tax base growth	15	23%	6	11%
No effect	8	12%	7	12%
Other	7	11%	2	4%
	N = 65		N = 57	

New Jersey

Response	Mentioned	%	1st Choice	%
Reduced operating exp.	9	41%	4	20%
Reduced cap. imp.	1	5%	0	0%
Raised local taxes	21	95%	14	70%
Increased fees, licenses	5	23%	0	0%
Used tax base growth	4	18%	2	10%
No effect	1	5%	0	0%
Other	2	9%	0	0%
	N = 22		N = 20	

ing expenses had increasingly been supported by revenue sharing funds, as indicated by the rise in use of the funds to maintain existing services.

New Jersey cities, facing no state constitutional or statutory tax limitation, overwhelmingly indicated (95 percent) raising local property taxes to make up for the loss of revenue sharing funds. This was most likely not an easy decision in a state with a highly disproportionate use of this unpopular tax. Since they had been less likely than California to use the funds for capital improvements, their second most frequent strategy was to reduce operating expenditures. Thus the response to the termination of General Revenue Sharing once again indicates that federal aid policies will, in their withdrawal as in their implementation, have effects which are greatly influenced by characteristics of the recipient governments, including state–local tax structure and revenue-raising limitations.[3]

The loss of General Revenue Sharing funds did contribute to a trend toward lower local government general fund balances, evidence of increasing fiscal strain. General fund balances declined from 4.4 percent in fiscal year 1986, the last full year of revenue sharing, to 3.4 percent in 1987. They stayed below 2 percent through 1994, a string unmatched since the years preceding passage of the program in 1972.[4] Local governments generally, and cities in particular, have also been forced to increase their use of the property tax. For municipal governments, property tax revenue grew nearly 10 percent as a percentage of personal income between fiscal year 1987 and fiscal 1992.[5]

Thus just as it had failed to meet expectations of dramatic impact upon passage, the termination of revenue sharing did not result in drastic changes at the local level. It did contribute, however, to greatly reduced local balances, an important measure of fiscal health. According to the survey data it slowed local government spending and contributed to an increase in property taxes and user fees, thus increasing the overall regressivity of the local revenue system.

THE DIFFICULTY OF ENACTING FEDERAL AID POLICY

The General Revenue Sharing experience offers a good example of the difficulties involved in enacting successful intergovernmental aid policy in a federal system, both generally and with respect to redistributive policy in particular. There were, as there often are, communication lapses and selective hearing during passage. State and local officials, desirous of the new form of federal aid, may not have been as candid about likely uses as they could have been. Members of Congress, eager to provide the funds and reap the political benefits, may not have wanted to recognize the likelihood of mundane uses when they were suggested. This led to vague, inflated, and even conflicting expectations, making the program's success difficult to evaluate and therefore its continuance difficult to defend. This dynamic can obviously be generalized to other federal aid programs, with the more discretion allowed, the more likely the lack of intergovernmental clarity.

Revenue sharing also provided an excellent example of how the need to get political support for a federal aid program may result in compromises that ultimately place a program at risk—by giving something to everyone but not enough to poor places, revenue sharing was unable to defend itself against either the charge that it sent funds to places without need or the criticism that not enough went to the truly needy units of government. While most agree that the national government should handle the redistributive role in our federal system,[6] the difficulty of enacting a program whose goal is to explicitly redistribute, by formula, among states and local governments, as opposed to individuals, is obvious both in the passage of revenue sharing and in the unsuccessful attempts to reform it.

Federal aid policy must also consider the great diversity of environments in which it will be implemented.[7] Characteristics of recipient governments, perhaps most directly those relating to revenue-raising ability and fiscal condition, will affect program impact. The early use of revenue sharing funds in New Jersey for property tax reduction is a vivid example of the important effect of state–local tax structure on the impact of a federal program, only one of several important subnational variables. To make sound policy, the many differences among states and among local governments must be understood and their effects anticipated in program development.

Decisions on the use of revenue sharing funds also showed that, when given discretion, local officials will usually budget in what is a cautious manner from *their* point of view. The desire to reduce uncertainty, and the potential negative fiscal and political effects of program termination, played an extremely important role in the use of General Revenue Sharing funds. Federal policy makers must realize and expect behavior like this in designing aid programs. There are differing incentives and constraints at work at the different levels of government, and state and local officials will not necessarily consider what would be in the best political or electoral interest of federal officials when implementing programs with few restrictions. In fact, they may use federal aid funds in such a way as to send a message to Washington regarding the intergovernmental aid environment—avoiding spending in certain areas to show, for example, that they will not take on financial burdens that they consider to belong to the federal government.

THE INTERGOVERNMENTAL LOBBY

The history of General Revenue Sharing parallels a rise and fall in the power of the intergovernmental lobby. That state and local officials were able to obtain passage of revenue sharing was a tribute to their strength in 1972; that they were unable to sustain it by the 1980s shows that their power had weakened. In fact, the debates over revenue sharing itself directly contributed to the intergovernmental lobby's loss of power.

Flush with success that was partly due to the expanding resources available to the federal government, the state and local lobby had started in the 1960s and 1970s to act like other interest groups, looking out only for their narrow self-interest and always asking for more (money and discretion, the only two things they could always agree upon), and using their ability to offer campaign support as barter.[8] They were no longer acting as elected officials who were part of a federal system of government, rising above parochial concerns in an attempt to develop better policy. In doing so, they forfeited an important moral ground. When the growth in federal resources slowed and campaign contributions became the key to access and influence, the intergovernmental lobby became less powerful.

This loss of power is evidenced by the fact that while the removal of revenue sharing from the federal grant landscape could be justified intellectually on deficit-reduction grounds, programs with weaker rationales survived. Political might often made right in the deficit-reduction battle, and the state–local lobby was overpowered. Lacking the political cache of the day—campaign contributions—they were unable to compete with stronger, better-funded, and more targeted interest groups. Revenue sharing also didn't even provide the political credit for members of Congress that categorical grants did.

Indeed, the debates over General Revenue Sharing actually directly resulted in a weakening, whether intentional or not, of the state–local lobby. With removal of state governments from the program in 1980, a wedge was driven between representatives of state and local governments, the latter fearful of losing their own share if they too vigorously protested the cut to states. That partnership has never returned to its previous status. And the consistent discussion of the issue of redistribution produced discord within the lobby groups representing local general-purpose governments.

The state and local lobby has claimed the Unfunded Mandates Relief Act as a victory, but the failure to get Congress to apply it to existing mandates or to require an extramajority override for new orders shows an inability of the lobby to get the preferred reform.[9] Also, it can certainly be argued that its passage was as much due to Republican ideology as a response to pressure from the public interest groups. After all, these groups had been complaining about unfunded mandates for years—why the sudden acceptance? The fact that the "Contract With America" had promised it is important.

Further, a leading authority on mandates has concluded that even in the first year of the law, significant new mandates and preemptions were passed, including an increase in the minimum wage for state and local government employees, alone estimated to cost them $1 billion over five years.[10] He further notes that Congress found its way around the law to impose several other significant mandates, including those relating to securities, immigration, and telecommunications reforms, and concluded that "State and local victories were largely achieved in modifying *how* new mandates were to be implemented, not in determining *whether* new mandates would be enacted."[11] This included modifications made to reduce the estimated cost of mandates so that they would not trigger the $50 million threshold. Among other potential prospective federal mandates on the policy horizon is the implementation of national education standards.

In general, the weakening of the state–local lobby is not a good thing for either federalism or federal aid policy making. While representatives of state and local governments clearly had become too interested in maximizing the amount of money they could obtain, all interest groups seek to maximize benefits from the federal government. At least state and local government interests represent elected officials who take a broader view and who are more accountable to the public than are most special interests. Their loss of influence reduces the impact on national government policy of an important source of information.

DEVOLUTION

The late 1990s have seen the devolution paradigm come to dominate discussions over federal aid. Programmatic and often fiscal responsibility is thought to be better placed, when feasible, at the subnational level. The legislative history of General Revenue Sharing and a weakened state–local lobby were important to the development of this perspective, while the lessons the revenue sharing experience offers for intergovernmental aid policy are particularly relevant.

General Revenue Sharing can be seen as the intellectual grandfather of the devolution movement. The passage of General Revenue Sharing in 1972 marked the first time that an overwhelming majority in Congress criticized its own grant policy, agreeing to the anti-Washington rhetoric which President Nixon had enunciated to help gain support for the program. For the first time in a long time, it was suggested that Washington didn't always know best—that narrow, categorical grants, with policy decisions made in Washington, didn't necessarily produce the best results. This sentiment would never again leave the policy arena, laying the foundation for Ronald Reagan's domestic cutbacks and a shifting of responsibilities and revenue raising from the center to the periphery. Indeed, outsider status has become a key element in nearly every presidential campaign since President Carter's in 1976.

The demise of revenue sharing spotlighted another extremely important aspect of the new reality of federal aid: Washington couldn't afford everything. Competing interests and programs, coupled with a slowing of economic growth and some dubious fiscal policies undertaken by the Reagan Administration, put enough pressure on the federal budget that something had to give. That it was revenue sharing, the most popular program ever for state and local officials, sent the strongest possible message that the glory days of federal aid were over.[12] Thus both the passage and termination of General Revenue Sharing set the stage for the devolutionary federal aid policies of the 1990s.

Devolution has occurred both explicitly and implicitly. The national government has reversed the growth in its nonentitlement aid to state and local governments; in real terms, it has fallen in every year except one since fiscal year 1978.[13] General Revenue Sharing was of course eliminated for states and then local governments, but programs such as the Safe Streets Act and the Comprehensive Employment and Training Act, among others, were also terminated.

Meanwhile there has been an implicit shift of responsibility and control to state and local governments, as they have taken on a greater role in the financing of services in our federal system. Between 1980 and 1990, state government own-source revenues grew from 9.4 percent of personal income to 10.8 percent, and from 6.9 percent to 8.3 percent for local governments, while dropping from 25 percent to 24.7 percent at the federal level.[14] As a result of these two trends—reduced federal aid and increased local revenue raising—federal aid to cities fell dramatically, from 0.21 per $1 of own-source revenues in fiscal year 1981 to 0.07 by fiscal year 1989.[15]

Recent federal aid policy primarily results from the marriage of the deficit reduction movement to public choice theory, both strongly held by the Republican Congress, producing the enhanced devolution movement of the 1990s.

Balancing the budget became the holy grail of federal policy in the late 1980s, as the deficit became an important symbol of what was wrong with Washington politics. It was a painfully obvious, easy-to-measure indicator of failed fiscal discipline, caused by the inability to say no to the demands of special interest groups. It was argued that as the public and state and local governments had to balance their checkbooks, so should Congress (false analogies, as most consumer debt is as high a percentage of income as was the federal deficit, while state and local governments have separate capital improvement budgets).

Joseph White and Aaron Wildavsky nicely summarized the position of importance the deficit reached:

> Political time is counted not in years but in issues; a political era is defined by the concerns that dominate debate and action, so that about other issues we ask: How does that affect . . . The budget has been to our era what civil rights, communism, the depression, industrialization, and slavery were at other times. Nor does the day of the budget show signs of ending. . . Year after year the key question has been, What will the president and Congress do about the deficit?[16]

Effect on the deficit did become the touchstone for most federal policy initiatives.

Many found the obsession with federal deficit reduction to be unjustified. Wildavsky, along with Naiomi Caiden, observed:

> During the first half of the 1990s, deficit panic turned into balanced budget hysteria. Hysteria is a state of alarm, not fully justified by the situation, in which emotion takes over from rationality. In conditions of political hysteria facts are not calmly assessed, consequences are not calculated, and public sentiments may be exploited for unrelated agendas.[17]

They continued:

> In times of rapid change and uncertainty, simplistic solutions, particularly those backed by authoritative opinions and doomsday scenarios, may have an irresistible appeal. The argument for a balanced budget is seductive in its simplistic virtue.[18]

Deficit reduction was to be the driving force behind the reform of many programs and the termination of others.

Devolution became a natural policy companion of federal deficit reduction. The notion of "government closer to the people" has always been an important part of American ideology (and ironically helped gain support for the enactment of General Revenue Sharing). Clearly, state and local governments had increased their administrative and fiscal capacities over the past twenty-five years, and were better able to handle and afford new responsibilities. Further, state and local elected officials had long sought more control over federal aid programs. Washington lawmakers saw these trends as an opportunity to eliminate some federal aid programs outright, and to reduce funding for others while increasing recipient discretion. The administrative savings from reduced oversight would presumably fill in for the reduced funding.[19]

While state and local officials welcomed the vote of confidence which devolution implies, they have been surprised by the magnitude of federal policy changes, enacted and proposed. They have always said they were willing to trade discretion for dollars, but the loss in dollars, especially at the local level, has been greater than anticipated. State and local governments clearly have preferred increased discretion with reduced funding in some programs, while retaining a consistent level of support in others. Most state officials balked at a proposed Medicaid block grant, for example, fearful of the financial burden it might entail. As with deficit reduction, the symbolic value of devolution may be easier to accept than its details.

Indeed, devolution seems to be driven as much by the pragmatic need for federal government deficit reduction as by any theory of federalism or federal aid. Whether it will lead to better policy remains to be seen. One negative effect of the implicit devolution has already been documented: the Center on Budget and Policy Priorities has reported a substantial increase in the regressivity of state tax systems.[20]

Since devolution involves increased discretion, its general design and implementation can benefit from a review of the experience with General Revenue Sharing. For example, communication between officials at the two levels of government should not be expected to be precise, for both factual and political reasons. Factually, officials at both levels will in many cases be moving into uncharted waters, only able to hypothesize impacts of increased discretion. Governors and other subnational officials may also resort for local political reasons to at least a little hyperbole as to their willingness and abilities. At the same time, they might want to under-report administrative savings for fear that the national government might further reduce its contribution; local chief executives followed this type of logic in refusing to use revenue sharing funds to replace those cut back in other federal program areas.

As with revenue sharing, vague and potentially conflicting goals are likely to emerge in an effort to build consensus. This can weaken both implementation and evaluation. Efforts should be made in the development of any devolutionary policy, as with any policy, to specify objectives in measurable terms.[21]

The great diversity of recipient governments in our federal system, particularly their fiscal disparities, is also likely to affect the impact of program changes and should be anticipated. State and local officials will further be motivated by the political dynamics of their respective states and localities, more so than by Washington's desires. Experience with revenue sharing showed that local officials in particular often budgeted those funds cautiously, as the desire to reduce uncertainty led officials to uses not anticipated in the nation's capital. As discretion in implementation of federal programs increases, all of these factors become more prominent in recipient response.

The 1995 reform of welfare provides examples of many of these issues. How will it be evaluated? Will success be measured by the number of individuals removed from the rolls, no matter what happens to them? Are widely differing state outcomes to be accepted? The latter is certainly likely to happen due to the varying political cultures and fiscal positions of states.[22] Once again, state officials will be more concerned with the fiscal and political impact of policy on *their* state, not how it helps or hurts federal policy makers. In revenue sharing there was a great reluctance to show Washington a willingness to use local funds to supplement what had been federal responsibilities, and that could certainly be repeated under welfare reform. As in the original New Federalism environment, program beneficiaries may be caught in the middle.

While all agreed to the basics of welfare reform, it took compromises—particularly hold-harmless provisions—to get the law enacted. As with revenue sharing, the diversity of impact among the states demanded changes from the original proposals to gain approval. These compromises may make evaluation and reauthorization difficult.

Finally, the intergovernmental lobby, as a whole, wasn't as involved in welfare reform as it might seem. The National Governors Association and National Conference of State Legislators were, for example, often put in a reactive position after policy proposals were developed by Republican congressional leaders conferring with Republican governors. And local officials had almost no say, although the needy often ultimately place demands on them.

As with termination of revenue sharing, federal deficit reduction was also an important factor in welfare reform. While it was often framed in terms of the failure of existing policy and the need to move decisions closer to the population served, there were large federal budget savings involved.[23] Deficit reduction, not better policy, may have been the driving force. One member of Congress admitted as much when he said house Budget Committee Chair John Kasich "gave us a number for welfare reform savings and said 'get there.'"[24]

Devolution of responsibility from the federal to state and local governments is a broad experiment. Success is therefore obviously dependent on the effectiveness of subnational implementation. The experience with the General Revenue Sharing program suggests that success may be more difficult to determine than is commonly held. The rhetoric of welfare reform, for example, while initially matched by a performance boosted by a thriving economy, may ultimately be difficult to attain, at least uniformly. Washington will then be faced with the decision to terminate its support, or recategorize, and perhaps even reentitle, the program.

PRESENT AND FUTURE REVENUE SHARING

Politics is always present in public policy making. Political dynamics allowed for the huge growth in the federal government role in this century, including the increase in federal aid to state and local governments. It helped in the enactment of General Revenue Sharing and was present at its demise. It is apparent in the 1990s' drive to devolve. To ignore politics in the development and explanation of public policy is to be naive. But to restrict policy alternatives to those deemed politically acceptable at any given moment is to forgo the opportunity to move debate forward and/or miss opportunities for change when they present themselves. Arguing against consideration of a program of revenue sharing due to federal budget deficits is an example of this shortsightedness.

Arguments for Revenue Sharing

Federal fiscal theorists have long maintained that the vertical and horizontal fiscal imbalances inherent in a federal system of government argue for unrestricted aid from the center to the periphery.[25] The budget experience in Washington over the past quarter century did nothing to weaken the strength of this theoretical perspective. Vertical fiscal imbalance exists. It is still easier for tax revenue to be raised nationally, due to lessened tax competition and a broader base, than at the state and local level, while state and local governments have a distinct advantage in tailoring benefits to local needs, a position more widely embraced now under devolution rhetoric than it has been in a long time.

The rich state–poor state, rich city–poor city problem of horizontal fiscal imbalance is as obvious as ever. In 1991, the most recent year available, state tax capacities ranged from lows of 68 percent of the national average in Mississippi and 77 percent in West Virginia to 134 percent in Wyoming and 130 percent in Connecticut.[26] The U.S. General Accounting Office reported in 1990 that "federal budget cuts helped to widen the fiscal gap between wealthier and poorer communities."[27] One analyst has concluded, "At the end of the decade [1980s], many big cities were significantly less well equipped to deliver adequate services to their residents at reasonable tax burdens than they had been two decades before."[28] Among other things, this situation threatens to weaken the great devolution experiment; differing fiscal capacities will affect ability to respond to the new responsibilities and distort competition, just as it does in the private sector. And governments can't go out of business.

There are many ways to make the intellectual case to bring back some form of revenue sharing. From the broadest perspective, a true federalist might argue that the only two inherent theoretical advantages a national government has are revenue-raising ability and information, the former due to lessened tax competition concerns, and the latter due to the fact that it is the only government in which people participate from each corner of the Union. Therefore, the purest form of federal aid would be unrestricted aid accompanied by information and ideas. As defender of the Constitution, federal courts would protect any violations by state and local governments of fundamental rights. This system would not be administratively perfect nor politically acceptable in Washington, but it is an interesting and arguable theoretical perspective on federal aid.[29]

Targeted, unrestricted aid could also fit with the current drive to devolve authority and its emphasis on economic incentives and competition. As noted, this grand experiment would more likely be successful if implemented in an environment where basic public services are adequate; if they are not, the experiment will be distorted by this important factor. Any competition is always distorted by inequality of resources.[30] Not all governments will be starting from anywhere near the same point fiscally in implementing welfare reform, for example. And while other devolutionary strategies such as urban empowerment and enterprise zones are good ideas, they will work best in cities where social and infrastructure needs have not, due to a lack of local fiscal capacity, fallen to a point where they deter economic activity.

It also seems contradictory that while many federal policy makers have accepted the evolution of the national government role as provider for the basic needs of individuals who lack resources, they hold the position that resource-poor local governments should fend for themselves and/or let their state governments be responsible for them. To take Congressman Wyler's question one step further, if subnational governments have such strong fiscal ability, why not let them be responsible for Social Security and Medicare? The distinction between needy individuals and needy governments is to a certain extent an artificial one, driven by historical events and politics as much as by policy merit.

The argument remains that since the federal government is responsible for the national economy, it should be responsible for the fallout from it. While Washington may take care of some of the income, housing, and medical needs of those suffering from economic dislocation, these individuals also put a strain on state and city services. If poverty is a national problem, local governments and central cities in particular, where its victims tend to congregate, should not have to pay a price disproportionate to their neighbors. Indeed, another flaw in the application of the market model to governments is the fact that no local government wants to compete to be the provider of choice to the poor.

The more narrow arguments for unrestricted federal aid include the simple fact that for whatever reason and whoever's fault, particular cities are struggling. They don't have the revenue authority or inclination, due to the fear of losing more taxpayers, to raise the revenues necessary to respond. Unrestricted aid from Washington, if properly targeted, could help with this problem.

There is also a strong argument to be made for unrestricted federal aid to state and local governments during recessionary times. It could produce spending which would stimulate the economy more quickly and perhaps more efficiently than spending from Washington.

The use of the federal budget deficit to argue against a program like revenue sharing has been narrow-minded and shortsighted. A deficit is not itself indicative of a lack of fiscal capacity; it reflects nothing more than the unwillingness of Congress to be fiscally responsible by balancing revenues and expenditures. The U.S. tax burden is one of the very lowest among Western industrialized nations; it could have been raised to balance the budget.

To say we cannot afford a program which seeks to even out differences in the fiscal capacities of state and local governments is to give short shrift to the importance of federalism and subnational governments, as opposed to other claimants to resources raised by the federal government. One could question whether the myriad of tax breaks given to corporations are more justifiable, or even more beneficial to the economy, than helping state and local governments provide basic services which benefit everyone, substituting revenue from the more progressive federal income tax for that of more regressive state and local tax instruments, or whether additional spending on defense is more important than helping cities provide clean, safe environments.

To reject on affordability grounds a program which seeks to even out the ability of state and local governments to provide basic services while protecting other beneficiaries is to hold this position.

The 1997 experience with deficit reduction also shows the short-sightedness of having most policy decisions driven by deficit numbers. Unexpected growth in the economy suddenly made it relatively easy to agree to a five-year plan to reduce the deficit to zero.

The fact that unrestricted aid is an important policy tool is confirmed by its continued use at the state level in the United States and its use in other nations. States use it to compensate for the varying fiscal capacities of their local units of government, to take pressure off the property tax, a tax with many sins, and to compensate for unfunded mandates.[31] It has consistently remained at 10 percent of all state aid to local governments and provided over $16 billion in fiscal year 1992.[32] Much of the largest category of state aid, aid for elementary and secondary education, is also nothing more than relatively unrestricted aid for this purpose. That aid nearly doubled in ten years, from roughly $61 billion in fiscal year 1982 to nearly $125 billion in fiscal year 1992.

A true federalist might argue that since the States think unrestricted aid is sound policy, the national government should follow. This logic of following the lead of the States was certainly at work in the balanced budget movement. While others would say that such aid obviates the argument for unrestricted federal aid, giving aid to their local units of government places uneven burdens on states due to their own varying fiscal capacities. Again, the national government has the greater revenue-raising ability. State legislatures may also, for political reasons, be less responsive to the most needy places, central cities in particular.

In other nations, revenue sharing is an integral part of federal fiscal systems. In Canada, for example, there is a program of unconditional revenue sharing called the Canadian Fiscal Equalization Program, "a constitutionally mandated unconditional block transfer program to support reasonably comparable levels of services at reasonably comparable levels of taxation."[33] Australia, Austria, and Germany have similar programs.

Revenue Sharing in Disguise

Unbeknownst to most, the concept of revenue sharing hasn't entirely disappeared from the federal government policy scene. The Local Partnership Act, initially introduced in 1992, was basically a revival of General Revenue Sharing. Attached to the 1994 Crime Bill, it sought to send $1.8 billion in unrestricted aid to general purpose local governments.[34] It was authorized but never funded—a perfect example of the ability of Congress to agree to the importance of unrestricted aid, but inability to fund it due to budget constraints.

The Local Government Law Enforcement Block Grant of 1995 is also a form of revenue sharing in thin disguise. Authorized at $2 billion a year for five years beginning in fiscal 1996, it received initial appropriations of $523 million.[35] Its main provisions basically allow the funds to be used for anything except tanks and aircraft.[36] Officials have recently come to realize that, as with revenue sharing, it will be very difficult to determine the actual impact of the funds. The law actually accomplishes more redistribution than revenue sharing did; by using the violent crime rate for allocational purposes, it sends disproportionately more money to needier places.

Maybe this, then, is the future of relatively unrestricted federal aid—to be periodically reborn under the rubric of the politically popular topic of the period. Forthcoming rationales might include elementary and secondary education or investment in infrastructure. In this way Congress can get credit for responding to a pressing concern, while state and local officials will receive funding more related to need and be able to use it fairly freely, even more so than under traditional block grants.

Should an actual revenue sharing-like policy of unrestricted aid be considered, it would be most easily justified if it were highly redistributive, going only to places with documented need. A good model would have it made permanent to avoid the distorting effect of uncertainty which revenue sharing had on local decisions, with cities being removed if they no longer met the criteria for need. A simple formula for allocation might rely on the number of people below the poverty line, multiplied by the cost of providing basic municipal services. The chief argument for a program for states, who have many more revenue options and much greater revenue ability than their local counterparts, would be to even out the effects of a downturn in the economy, so-called countercyclical or anti-recessionary aid.

To make the case for unrestricted aid in a federal system is not to expect its return. Political dynamics and the current political environment do not favor the return of a federal revenue sharing program. But closer consideration of the politics of its demise, and a reexamination of the policy issues raised in attempts to reform it, argue for reconsideration of a broad policy idea that still makes sense.

CONCLUSION

As stated at the outset of this chapter, knowledge of the history of General Revenue Sharing is crucial to understanding the changed environment of U.S. intergovernmental relations in the 1990s.

There are so many ironies surrounding the history of General Revenue Sharing. The program's passage was the high point of state and local government cooperation and success in lobbying. Yet its reauthorizations and the removal of states drove a wedge between representatives of these two levels of government, with lingering effects, while attempts to change revenue sharing's formula to redistribute more to needy local governments exposed splits within the local government lobby. Introduced as a program which would return power to state and local governments, General Revenue Sharing was terminated because its beneficiaries did not have enough power against other claimants in the federal budgetary (deficit-cutting) arena. Heralded as a devolution of power itself, its reconsideration has been argued to be out of line with the 1990s trend toward devolution, and its public choice theory dynamic. Beneficiary of early anti-Washington sentiment in its passage, it fell prey to the anti-Washington sentiment encompassed by the drive to balance the federal budget. Enacted to a great extent to remedy what were seen as the fiscal inadequacies of subnational government, it served as the transition piece from a majority of federal intergovernmental aid being dedicated to governmental purposes to a majority taking care of the needs of indigent individuals.

It could be argued that General Revenue Sharing was not only a victim of timing when it was terminated, but more broadly was doomed by its date of birth. Had the program been in place for decades before budget pressures mounted in the 1970s and 1980s, it might have been better institutionalized. That our Constitution is so old, with the result that our federal fiscal system has evolved rather than ever been re-rationalized, worked against this new form of federal aid. "Last in, first out" can happen in federal aid programs, too.

There remains a logic for a system of unrestricted federal aid. Whether to help poor cities provide a basic level of services while reducing the overall regressivity of the federal fiscal system or to help states struggle through recessionary troughs, revenue sharing could once again have a place in the U.S. grant system.

Ideas are important in policy development. Deficit reduction ruled the late 1980s and most of the 1990s; devolution, initially prodded by deficit reduction, appears ready to become the "idea who's time has come" for the transition to the next century. But should devolution produce too many victims, whether governmental or individual, pressure could once again build for fairness.[37] Should that happen, a new form of revenue sharing, informed by the experience of the federal General Revenue Sharing program, might be part of an appropriate policy response.

NOTES

1. See Anna Marie Cammisa, *Governments As Interest Groups: Intergovernmental Lobbying and the Federal System* (Westport, Conn: Praeger, 1995).

2. Lindsey Gruson, "End of Federal Revenue Sharing Creating Financial Crises in Many Cities," *New York Times*, January 31, 1987, p. 6.

3. These findings on city response to termination of revenue sharing were supported by other studies. See, for example, Khi V. Thai and David Sullivan, "Impact of Termination of General Revenue Sharing on New England Local Government Finance," *Public Administration Review* 49, Jan/Feb 1989:61–67; Paul R. Dommel and Keith P. Rasey, "Coping with the Loss of General Revenue Sharing in Ohio," *Public Budgeting and Finance* 9, Autumn 1989, pp. 43–51; Vincent L. Marando, "General Revenue Sharing: Termination and City Response," *State and Local Government Review*, Fall 1990, pp. 98–107; John P. Forrester and Charles J. Spindler, "Assessing the Impact on Municipal Services of the Elimination of General Revenue Sharing, *State and Local Government Review*, Spring 1990, pp. 73–83; Brent S. Steel, Nicholas P. Lovrich, and Dennis L. Soden, "A Comparison of Municipal Responses to the Elimination of Federal General Revenue Sharing in Florida, Michigan, and Washington," *State and Local Government Review* 21, no. 3 (1989): 106–115.

4. Calculated from U.S. Advisory Commission on Intergovernmental Relations, *Significant Features of Fiscal Federalism—vol. 2, 1994* (Washington, DC: ACIR), tables 33 and 43, p. 66 and 78.

5. Calculated from U.S. Department of Commerce, Bureau of the Census, *Census of Governments*, vol. 4, "Finances of Municipal and Township Governments," 1987 and 1992.

6. See, for example, Paul E. Peterson, *City Limits* (Chicago: University of Chicago Press, 1981).

7. For an excellent early discussion of this point, see Jeffrey B. Pressman and Aaron Wildavsky, *Implementation: How Great Expectations in Washington are Dashed in Oakland* (Berkeley, CA: University of California Press, 1975).

8. See B.J. Reed, "The Changing Role of Local Advocacy in National Politics," *Journal of Urban Affairs* 5 (Fall): 287–298.

9. See Paul Posner, *The Politics of Unfunded Mandates* (Washington, DC: Georgetown University Press, 1998).

10. Paul L. Posner, "Unfunded Mandate Reform: 1996 And Beyond," *Publius—The Journal of Federalism* 27, no. 2, Spring 1997, pp. 53–71.

11. Posner, "Unfunded Mandate Reform. . . .," p. 1.

12. Charles H. Levine and James A. Thurber, "Reagan and the Intergovernmental Lobby: Iron Triangles, Cozy Subsystems and Political Conflict," ed. Allan J. Cigler and Burdett A. Loomis, *Interest Group Politics*, 2nd ed. (Washington, DC: Congressional Quarterly Press, 1986): 202–220.

13. U.S. Advisory Commission on Intergovernmental Relations, *Significant Features of Fiscal Federalism, vol. 2* (Washington, DC: ACIR, 1994), table C, p. 9.

14. U.S. Advisory Commission on Intergovernmental Relations, *Significant Features of Fiscal Federalism, vol. 2* (Washington, DC: ACIR, 1994), table 20, p. 46.

15. U.S. Advisory Commission on Intergovernmental Relations, *Significant Features of Fiscal Federalism, vol. 2* (Washington, DC: ACIR, 1988), p. 84.

16. Joseph White and Aaron Wildavsky, *The Deficit and the Public Interest* (Berkeley, CA: University of California Press, 1990), pp. *xv–xvi.*

17. Aaron Wildavsky and Naiomi Caiden, *The New Politics of the Budgetary Process,* 3rd ed. (New York: Longman, 1997), p. 293.

18. Wildavsky and Caiden, *The New Politics. . .,* p. 293.

19. This is similar to the argument President Nixon used when he announced proposed cutbacks in federal aid programs after General Revenue Sharing was enacted. He said that state and local officials could, where they deemed it wise, use new funds to replace those cut back.

20. See Nicholas Johnson and Iris Lav, "Are State Taxes Becoming More Regressive?" Center on Budget and Policy Priorities, Washington, DC, October 29, 1997.

21. See Bruce A. Wallin, "The Need for a Privatization Process: Lessons from Development and Implementation," *Public Administration Review* 57, no. 1, Janauary/February 1997.

22. See Bruce A. Wallin, "Federal Cutbacks and the Fiscal Condition of the States," *Publius* 26, no. 3 (1996).

23. The same is true for most proposed reforms of Medicaid.

24. Congressman Martin Meehan to the author, January 15, 1996.

25. See Break, *Financing Government in. . .*

26. *Significant Features* Table 98, p. 182.

27. U.S. General Accounting Office, *Federal–State–Local Relations: Trends of the Past Decade and Emerging Issues* (Washington, DC: GAO, 1990), p. 5.

28. Helen F. Ladd, "Big-City Finances," in *Big-City Politics, Governance, and Fiscal Constraints,* ed. George E. Peterson (Washington, DC: The Urban Institute Press, 1994): 201–269, at 201.

29. Bruce A. Wallin, "Toward a Pure Theory of Federal Aid," paper presented at the Annual Meeting of the American Society for Public Administration, San Francisco, CA, July 18–21, 1993.

30. On this point see William H. Oakland, "Recognizing and Correcting for Fiscal Disparities: A Critical Analysis," in *Fiscal Equalization For State and Local Government Finance,* ed. John E. Anderson (Westport, CT: Praeger, 1994): 1–19, at p. 8.

31. U.S. Advisory Commission on Intergovernmental Relations, *The State of State–Local Revenue Sharing* (Washington, DC: ACIR, 1980), p. 2.

32. U.S. Advisory Commission on Intergovernmental Relations, *Significant Features of Fiscal Federalism, 1994, Vol. 2,* table D, p. 10.

33. Anwar Shah, "Intergovernmental Fiscal Relations in Canada: An Overview," in *Macroeconomic Management and Fiscal Decentralization,* ed. Jayanta Roy (Washington, DC: The World Bank, 1995): 233–255, at 239.

34. Title 31, Chapter 67 of U.S. Code. See Don Nickles, "Anti-Crime Proposal," *Congressional Press Releases* (Washington, DC: Federal Document Clearing House, Inc., 1994), August 19.

35. U.S. House of Representatives, "Conference Report to Accompany H.R. 3610," 104th Congress, 2nd Session, Report 104–863, September 28, 1996.

36. See "Program Title 16.592 Local Law Enforcement Block Grants Program," *Catalog of Federal Domestic Assistance 1996 Update*.

37. See Wallin, "Federal Cutbacks. . ."

Appendix: Cities in Survey

CALIFORNIA CITIES

Alameda
Alhambra
Anaheim

Bakersfield
Bellflower
Berkeley
Buena Park
Burbank

Carson
Chula Vista
Compton
Concord
Costa Mesa

Daly City
Downey

El Cajon
El Monte

Fremont
Fresno
Fullerton

Garden Grove
Glendale

Hawthorne
Hayward
Huntington

Inglewood

Lakewood
Long Beach
Los Angeles

Modesto
Mountain View
Norwalk

Oakland
Ontario
Orange
Oxnard

Palo Alto
Pasadena
Pico Rivera
Pomona

Redondo Beach
Redwood City
Richmond
Riverside

Sacramento
Salinas
San Bernardino
San Diego
San Francisco
San Jose
San Leandro
San Mateo
Santa Ana
Santa Barbara
Santa Clara

NEW JERSEY CITIES

Asbury Park
Atlantic City

Bayonne
Bloomfield
Bridgeton

Camden
Cherry Hill
Clifton

East Orange
Edison
Elizabeth

Hamilton Township
Hoboken

Irvington

Jersey City

Lakewood
Long Branch

Middletown Township
Millville

Neptune Township
Newark
New Brunswick

Orange

CALIFORNIA CITIES

Santa Monica Vallejo
Santa Rosa Ventura
Simi Valley
South Gate West Covina
Stockton Westminster
Sunnyvale Whittier

Torrance

NEW JERSEY CITIES

Parsipanny Troy Hills
Passaic
Paterson
Perth Amboy
Plainfield

Trenton
Union City
Union Township
Vineland
Woodbridge Township

Index